PERSONAL FREEDOM
AND
FINANCE

SHORT FOUNDATIONAL DISCUSSIONS ON PERSONAL ECONOMICS AND FINANCE FOR TODAY'S YOUNG ADULTS

4tNox U

BROOKS LEVONITIS
EDITOR-IN-CHIEF

PERSONAL FREEDOM AND FINANCE

SHORT FOUNDATIONAL DISCUSSIONS ON PERSONAL ECONOMICS & FINANCE FOR TODAY'S YOUNG ADULTS

(Resource Information Included)

FIN 001 : Personal Freedom and Finance

via

4t Nox U

'Unlocking the Vaults of Knowledge'
...one person at a time

Whereas complexity confuses, simplicity clarifies; therefore, 4t Nox U strives to lay strong foundations and promote the fundamentals of personal economics & finance so that learning is applicable, actionable, and scalable.

4t Nox U is a personal finance web site dedicated to knowledge and application. 4t Nox is the business education division of Thespis Media, Ltd. Co. (www.thespismedia.com), a leader in new media training, education and professional development. Thespis Media/4t Nox is the creator of Life Finances - the award-winning 3D, virtual personal finance curriculum/courseware (blended & digital) for upper level students – and its accompanying Teacher's Dashboard – a powerful digital teacher's aide (online tracking and administration, and online delivery, grading, averaging, recording, and reporting of course assessments).

PREAMBLE

Financial prudence, diligence and discipline are keys to personal freedom. I have met very few young men and women who set out into adulthood expecting to retreat back home or become wards of the state. Mankind desires, innately, to be free and independent. No other group embodies this fact like young adults; they have so many dreams to be fulfilled and so many missions to accomplish, and they have the energy to charge ahead ambitiously. Unfortunately certain philosophies are promulgated which attempt to suppress man's natural state and pursuits. And a lack of knowledge and discipline (sometimes fate) allow this primary yearning to dissipate quietly, subtly pushing man to succumb to an untoward condition of dependence. This discussion for young adults aims to encourage them to define success as they envision it and to take advantage of the opportunities before them; hopefully, it helps set a solid foundation so that additional knowledge and further wisdom can be obtained when sought and with a proper understanding, and so that freedom and independence can be confidently pursued, attained and maintained. The "American Dream" cannot be achieved independent of independence.

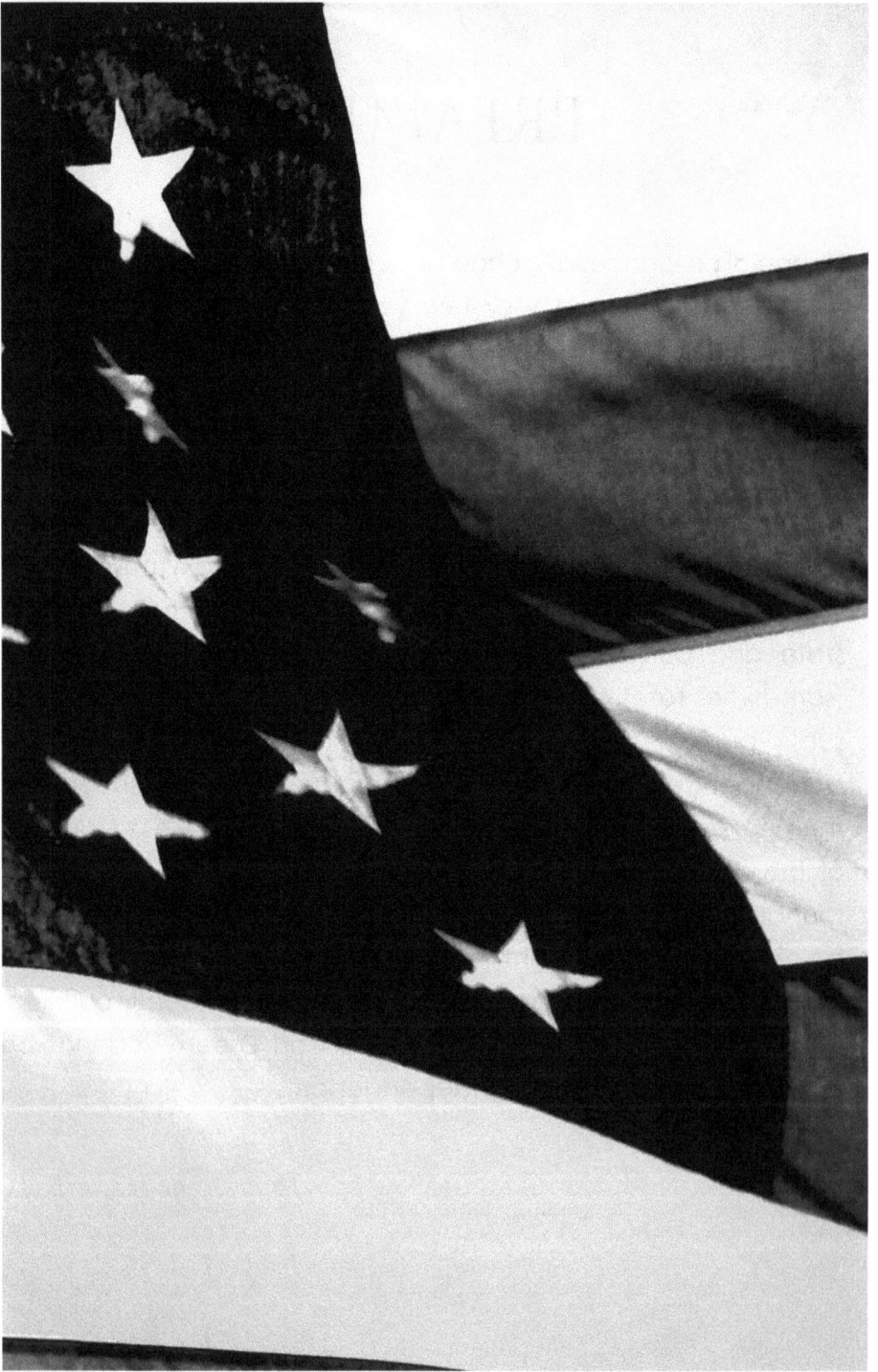

This book is dedicated to young adults whose futures are just getting started and are ever so bright. You yearn for the opportunity to make your marks in the world. I encourage you to do so with a sense of urgency and unyielding determination - Life is shorter than you imagine and there are no mulligans. In the end you will either say, "I am glad I did" or "I wish I would have". Which statement will you make?

"I am only one, but I am one. I can't do everything, but I can do something. The something I ought to do, I can do. And by the grace of God, I will."

Grant Teaff c. 1980 (likely quoting Edward Everett Hale)

To your future,

TABLE OF CONTENTS

DISCUSSION 1: INTRODUCTION

Grasping the foundation

1.1: Purpose – Economic freedom is a requirement for free peoples.

This primer is focused on making basic fundamental principles understandable and accessible to a majority of young adults. Finance and economics can be very complex academic subject matter. Thankfully, achieving personal finance success is less rigorous, yet it will require a certain level of discipline one cannot get around. Eventual success will be achieved by picking up nuggets of wisdom from multiple sources, diligent planning, and, of course, self discipline.

There are three main reasons why we as a society have become less than financially successful: 1) a lack of education; 2) a lack of discipline; and, 3) certain groups among us (industry groups, non-profits, and bureaucrats) profit, financially and politically, from the perpetuation of dependence and its unfortunate deleterious affects on our citizenry, and therefore they fight overtly and covertly for policies that maintain or increase the numbers of people who lack independence – it has become a cottage industry for some enterprising souls. Of course there are those who will always need assistance of some kind (this real need opens the door to profiteers), and the harsh reality is that sometimes bad things happen to good people – an unfortunate reality that could quickly befall any one of us, and which should be viewed through empathetic eyes, if not through sympathetic personal experiences. While a financial plan cannot completely eliminate the hand of fate, that is no excuse to be irresponsible and defer appropriate planning.

4t Nox U seeks to assist in addressing reason number 1 above (and by reading this primer you are taking personal responsibility for your own education, which is laudable and required); reason 2 must be dealt with on a personal level (laziness or apathy will exact painful consequences which many times force change); and, reason 3 will naturally die as more people pursue education and personal independence and achieve economic freedom.

Practically, financial/economic freedom is a requirement of a free people. Not to get too philosophical but for our republic to survive as the shining light on a hill it must be inhabited by men and women who understand the basic principles of freedom, and the negative consequences of dependence. Men who have economic freedom will not easily give up political freedom; men who are dependent, either upon the state, state-affiliated enterprises, or others, often times willingly give up some freedoms, mistakenly, out of perceived necessity. It is a very simple concept and one which we can easily observe.

Summary – Freedom is not free; it requires payment in discipline and sacrifice. Choose to be one of those who enjoy independence, and not one who gets sucked into the 'dependence system' that exists to grow its ranks, and thus its financial and political power. Education and hard work are your keys to economic liberty. This primer is a great educational resource as you get started on your own independent path.

1.2: Financial Basics – You don't have to start big to end big.

Too many young people believe they are behind the financial "eight ball" because they don't start with a pile of cash. "It takes money to make money" is true, but the quip does not mean that only those with money can make money. Don't be duped by that wrong-headed, almost victim-like mentality.

Those without money must do one of two things – earn more than they spend and use the surplus funds as the "money to make money", the seed capital if you will; or, engage those who do have money to give them some. Now, the second plan does not refer to confiscation and redistribution. Rather, and contrary, it embodies the ideal of free-market capitalism. If you have a great idea, one that will provide a return on invested capital, you only need convince one with capital to back you and your idea. If it is a good idea, it very well may find one with money who would be willing to invest. While not everyone with money makes a good investment partner, you don't need everyone to invest. You only need find one or two good partners. Many of those with capital appreciate the opportunity to invest in ventures which will provide a decent return on capital above and beyond whatever they deem a risk-free return. I believe Facebook ($100B) was "founded" with an initial $15,000 capital injection, and it did end up returning slightly more than the then current risk-free rate to the investment partner (co-founder Eduardo Saverin).

The first thing a new entrant into the "economic system" can do is generate surplus funds. You may not be an entrepreneur and/or you may not have any good ideas. That doesn't mean you cannot use basic financial principles to increase your net worth. You, too, should make money work for you, even if it is only $50 per month. Compounding interest is a powerful concept. We will discuss it further in the Investment sections, but earning solid rates of return over a significant amount of time can turn the most modest of investments into a substantial nest egg, large enough that you can declare yourself independent – freedom, inherently, is a main objective of most young people.

Summary – Don't spend more than you earn. Save the surplus funds and use as seed capital or investment funds. Take advantage of the system in which you live, free-market capitalism, and engage capitalists (your partners, teammates) to fulfill your entrepreneurial goals.

1.3: Economic Basics – Build a personal fortress balance sheet.

The section title, Economic Basics, does not refer to classical supply and demand curves. We are talking about personal economics, daily choices that impact your situation; shrewd purchasing, needs versus wants, creating economic value, and the like, and for this book, understanding and applying the FREEDOM INDICATOR (FI).

Some of these personal economic principles will be addressed in future sections; however, I would encourage you to go ahead and forward to Appendix A and view the FI. The idea is not to slap down a concrete number that denotes wealth or someone else's idea of success or financial freedom. Everyone will have a different number that works for them, depending on life-long goals, familial obligations, cost of living disparities, etc. The FI does provide a framework that will help you simplify your main goal to become financially free. Many times complexity reduces focus and effectiveness. By providing a very simple framework, you can narrow your focus and determine what you need to do – economic decisions - to become independent. This determination will be required to build your balance sheet into a personal financial fortress.

Summary – Your balance sheet will determine how financially independent you become. Everyone's FI is different, but you should determine a number and commit to do what is necessary to meet that goal.

1.4: Challenge – Seek your significance.

Many times people decide that a topic is too difficult to delve into or that spending valuable X-box time learning something applicable to real life isn't worth it. Then there are those who do take the time to learn something new only to either shelve the recently-obtained knowledge (usually never applying it with any modicum of success or longevity) or abandon it when things get a little tougher than expected. This lack of focus, discipline and tenacity is, bluntly, immature and a precursor to future individual failures, and over time, if widespread, a recipe for cultural decay. We need a citizenry which is well-educated, dogged in its determination, and tough enough to fight through eventual set backs, as they will come surely as the sun will rise in the east tomorrow morning.

I challenge you to not only read this book, but also to internalize its concepts and apply them systematically in your life. Additionally, I want to challenge your mettle, if you will, with a simple commitment prior to your first major obstacle, of which you will be confronted with many. Nothing significant is easily attained; if it could be achieved effortlessly everyone would succeed and its value would be, rightly, diminished. Determining to become and remain independent is simple in theory but herculean in practice, and it is a significant and honorable quest. Today, right now, make a commitment to yourself that you will attack and overcome each obstacle that attempts to prevent you from becoming independent and free. By taking a stand prior to the event and preparing yourself mentally, you will be better prepared to manage the difficult times calmly and rationally. Mostly, you will be less likely to let yourself down. Tough times will come. Fighting through to make an extra buck isn't very compelling; overcoming difficult circumstances to reach a monumental and even transcendent objective is quite compelling.

Personal freedom is a transcendent cause. You need to, first, understand the weight of this concept, then believe such a cause is a priority for you, and, finally, accept the challenge. Those who are apathetic will live with unintended consequences; those who dispute the importance of individual freedom do not fully comprehend America's historic DNA and may end up fighting for some mistaken virtue of universal dependence. But, those who are able to understand the importance and implications of such simple yet weighty concepts as individual liberty and financial freedom will determine to make the necessary choices to achieve their personal FI. By doing so they will be able to move, speak, and give freely, without a dependent restraint which suppresses one's unique desires. Dependence constricts; independence (especially the journey toward) unleashes the power of the human spirit - I hope you choose the latter, on your own terms, in your own context, for all the right reasons.

Significance is a much more important concept than the less-than-inspiring idea of financial success. In theory, once one achieves economic freedom one can focus on pursuing things of significance. However, we are not guaranteed another day, so execute your significance plans as soon as possible and in conjunction with your FI plans, knowing that in time when you reach your FI goal you will be able to dedicate even more resources to those things which you determine to be worthy of your efforts (significance isn't something you necessarily seek to gain, it is usually received as a silent badge for your many acts of thoughtfulness and selflessness).

Point – Do not wait until you have "made it" before investing in other people; do all you can when you can and while you can because time really is short. Financial success is only a means, the journey is what really matters and the end results (your impact on others) are what determine lasting significance.

Summary – Life is short, make yours count, now. Don't let things that seem like insurmountable obstacles derail your plans – see them as challenges that can and will be overcome. Do not wait until you have reached your FI to begin making strides toward defining your significance. Plan like you will live forever; make decisions of significance like you are on borrowed time and don't know when the principal will be called - A sense of urgency will drive positive actions. Financial success may or may not come exactly as you have planned; regardless, invest in other people, in things that will not return to dust, in becoming significant in your own way and in your own time.

DISCUSSION 2:
EDUCATION

Education is very much an input into your personal finance equation, as your ability to earn a living will directly impact your budget

<u>2.1: Relevant Education – The 21st century is the age of individualization, customization, and on-demand learning.</u>

If you are a recent graduate who has just taken a number of final exams, you are probably ready, understandably, to lay the thought of a discussion on education aside. If you have been out of school awhile the thought of going back is likely painful. But, let's view education from a slightly different paradigm going forward. (It will make the discussion more palatable.) I suggest you see 21st century education as on-demand life-long learning from anywhere at anytime at your own pace versus a schoolhouse with textbooks, hardwood desks and a synchronous schedule. Hopefully, this prism of personalized education provides a more encouraging outlook for your future educational endeavors because the reality is that your willingness to continuously update your skills will make a significant impact on your future – personal, economic, and financial.

Education comes in multiple forms; classical, traditional, religious, theoretical, applied, trial & error, hard-knocks, etc. Most students today, though less so than at any time in modern history, attend a traditional primary and secondary education (K-12), and then go the applied route (apprenticeships, military training, and entry-level positions). Over the last 50 years our society has pushed for more advanced education because a diploma/certificate/degree imply a certain "smarts" (level of competence) and because an information economy requires a knowledgeable workforce. And it probably doesn't hurt as studies show that people with advanced education earn substantially more over a lifetime. Of course, all forms of education are helpful and relevant to a certain extent. Unfortunately, in our quest to develop more educational opportunities and a more "educated" workforce, it seems we may have slightly missed the mark.

We have spent substantially more money on education, publicly and privately, over the last generation than we ever have in any previous generation; yet, we really haven't seen a reciprocal outcome. An increasing number of our high school and college graduates are ill-prepared to take the next step; i.e., employers are surprised at the wanting skill set of applicants, and college remediation courses are filled with more students than ever. We have college freshmen who passed Algebra I, Algebra II, and Geometry in high school, but they are not qualified to enter an introductory College Algebra class. And this remediation problem is prevalent in Language Arts/English Comp almost as much as in mathematics. Add to this lack of readiness student loan debt (Over $1 Trillion!) which is higher than at any time in history – it is a conundrum on many levels. Worse yet these students have less purchasing power than my generation, and a much worse "balance sheet" right out of the gate. Something has gone awry in our system.

Some of you will feel this pinch very soon. You may not know the underlying reasons for your hardship, but you will know that something didn't work as you expected. The bad news is that you don't get any "redos." The good news is that as you understand this situation you will be able to take action now to right the ship sooner rather than later. I will present two action steps in the next few paragraphs and encourage you to act upon them – set life goals and design a strategy to meet them.

Initially, if you don't have a strong desire to go in a certain direction, take some serious time, ask yourself difficult questions, probe your heart and really figure out what you want to do. It is crucial that you get excited about your future. No one else, outside of possibly your parents, will give it a lot of thought. How pathetic if you just mull through your one shot at success and significance, if you mindlessly wander through a bare existence, if you are never inspired or never inspire others, if you never have a positive impact on someone else. Alternatively, how cool if you dare to do great things.....<u>Man in the Arena</u>

Life will present many difficulties along your journey. If you know what awaits you on the other side, you will have the drive to persevere through those tough times. Otherwise, you will be more easily disheartened and unmotivated to plow through obstacles which will inevitably arise. Hopeful people are excited and motivated people; those without hope are sad, unmotivated, and even miserable. Which camp are you in now? Which camp do you want to be in?

I am not encouraging you to design a career path yet. Without a strong desire planning a path may be a moot point. Determine what you want to accomplish with your life and then proceed to goal setting. Once you know the "what and why", the "how" really doesn't matter. Having a plan is better than not having a plan, but when you are passionate about your life's work you will figure out the "how" one way or another. And many times you will need to adjust your tactics as circumstances dictate – focus on the why and I am confident the how will become clear.

Where do you see yourself in 10 years, in 20 years? Once you are passionate about your life's work, sit down and design a long-term strategy to meet your goals. And this leads in to the title of this section – Relevant Education. If you would really like to pursue a career within a charitable organization so that you can help underprivileged children, you need to determine how closely your skill set and desire merge. Did you get a degree in history, and then only on deep reflection since graduation decide you wanted to dedicate the next 10 years to helping kids? If so, you need a plan of attack that gets your foot in the door. Since I am confident if this is where your passion leads you will figure out the "how", I will not spend a lot of time on tactics, but I do want to lay out a couple of scenarios to get you thinking correctly if your passion is not necessarily aligned with your current education. (If you have always wanted to become a medical doctor, a general practitioner, and you are planning on getting into medical school to fulfill your lifelong dream, then I don't think much else needs to be said. You are locked in and ready for the next step.)

History major's possible tactical move: Set a meeting with the executive director of an organization that helps underprivileged children and share your passion, share your story of how you came to know "the what and why". Explain that you have a degree in history which may not be directly applicable to the field, but that you are a good public speaker and that, as an example, you worked band summer camps during college breaks as the assistant activities director. You would be willing to intern with the communications manager or the events coordinator so that your current skill set could be of value to the organization. Additionally, you would be willing to attend professional development seminars or on-line short courses applicable to fundraising for non-profit organizations – relevant education. In return you only ask that after a certain time period, say three months, you would be considered for an entry level job.

I am sure you get the gist of the solution. Offer your current skill set and then offer to learn whatever you can that will add value to the organization. The group may need an accountant. If you hate math, are horrible at math, and have no desire to go into accounting, obviously this wouldn't be a good fit. You don't want to harm the organization! But, if you are more than capable of learning non-profit accounting, even though it isn't the perfect position, at least your willingness to "take one for the team" right out of the gate will get you in the door to work for an organization that is serving underprivileged kids – your passion. Once a part of the team, and a valuable part, new opportunities will become available in time.

One more example, in the same vein - maybe you really want to be a video game developer. Are you a programmer? "No." Are you a designer? "No." Are you a good player? "Excellent, I spent most of my first five years of college playing MMOGs." Great, you have relevant experience, so now apply to a company that makes video games and tell them why you would be the very best alpha/beta game tester they could ever find. (Obviously, this is a highly-sought, competitive entry-level position!) Yes, maybe you only took one Intro to Programming course and you have a math education degree, but tell them why you are passionate about online gaming, and that you are an expert in one of their product lines. Tell them that you would love to intern for a year within a testing group as you learn (relevant education) MS SQL, C+, etc. Share your passion for their industry, company, and product suites, find out what they need, and work diligently to become a valuable member of the organization. Because it will take a substantial amount of work and sacrifice, you must be passionate about the work, which is why I encourage you to take some time and really determine what you want to do.

It's not as easy as I have proposed. Hopefully you didn't expect easy; if so, someone wasn't completely upfront with you. I mean, how many online game publishers are there in Topeka, KS? Can you really afford to go to California and live off an intern's wages (free to minimum wage)? If so, maybe it is not such a bad idea. If not, maybe you should focus on developing your new skill set before making any big moves. Does this mean going back to school? Maybe, maybe not. Traditional education is good, but could you learn what is necessary more cheaply and faster via the internet, an apprenticeship, or an internship? If traditional education is the right path, take it. If there are alternative routes, and there usually are, don't be afraid to pursue a different form of education. You may have to take a night shift job as a stocker at the local Wal-Mart or Home Depot as you learn your new skills. That would be a great time to think through multiple skins, levels, functions of your first iPhone game app, as you pay the bills while learning. If you are passionate about the "what and why", you will figure out the "how".

Summary – Relevant education is important to your future. You may or may not have received the formal education necessary to pursue your real passion in life. Don't let this minor roadblock stop you. There are so many options available with regard to relevant education it would be foolish not to figure out how to exploit its availability. The 21st century really is the dawn of a whole new paradigm in "education." While on-demand, fully-customized training isn't a reality just yet, relevant education is nearly ubiquitous, readily accessible, highly flexible, and many times extremely efficient – take advantage of these historic changes.

2.2: Philosophies of Education – Teach to think broadly (Classical) versus teach to do a specific job (Industrial).

At a high level there are two philosophies of education: Classical and Industrial. Classical education usually focuses a student's coursework on liberal arts, the study of great books, and philosophical thinking. The aim is to become a broad thinker who can grasp any topic from a strong foundational position. If you know how to think and reason, you should be able to apply a rigorous intellectual process to any problem/situation and work to a well-thought solution/conclusion. An Industrial education would be more discipline specific. If you are planning to go into marketing, you would focus much of your time on marketing classes. Understanding the philosophical battle between Locke and Hobbes would be, at most, tertiary versus understanding price and positioning and studying Starbucks' marketing strategy.

Obviously there are merits to both philosophies. Our goal is not to engage in this debate directly. I just want you to understand where you sit on this lever. By knowing your strengths and weaknesses, you know what to emphasize to whom, and you know what to work on.

Should we just educate to fill a workforce? I don't think so. Should we not teach any application of hard skills? Of course not. It is very valuable to be able to draw from a broad knowledge base and think outside the box. As well, it is quite valuable to know how Starbucks convinced people to pay $3 for a strong cup of coffee which could be made quickly at home for 20 cents. There are sensible viewpoints on each side of this educational spectrum. I believe both philosophies are important for one to be successful in the global Information Age. In a sense, when and how one is educated or trained are more important to me than if (because uneducated / untrained / unskilled is <u>not</u> an option).

Summary - Classical or Industrial education? Regardless, you need to understand your background and the corresponding strengths and weaknesses developed by such. You should strive to enhance your strengths and fill in your weaknesses.

2.3: Continuing Education – Pursue interests and opportunities.

Again, to reiterate my educational mantra – Learning is a life-long endeavor, and it will have a significant impact on your future. It is in your best interest to buy into this idea sooner rather than later, if for only one very important reason..... because I'm right. It is hard to go wrong by committing to self improvement.

If you do not know your strengths and weaknesses, invest in a sound self-evaluation inventory that will enable you to realize your strengths, recognize your weaknesses, and prepare a plan to address those things which need improvement.

Successful people appreciate those who know their strengths and weaknesses, know how to compensate where necessary, and those young professionals who have taken the time to plan, execute, measure, and evaluate a self-improvement plan. It is hard not to respect a person who is willing to go the extra mile; your efforts will separate you from the masses, and they will get recognized.

Read and Reflect (then commit to continuing education) -

In our Global Information Age things are changing quite dramatically. You must now compete with brilliant, aggressive all-stars from Ukraine, India, China, South Africa, Israel, Estonia, Chile, etc. These young people are working overtime to improve their lot in life. This is not 1950s America where many could graduate high school, get a job in a manufacturing plant making a good salary/benefits, and plan on a secure long-term career with a solid pension in retirement. We still manufacture, quite well in many places, and there will always be a need for the equivalent of quality machinists, electricians, welders, mechanics, etc. However, your computer products were probably manufactured by a contract manufacturer in Asia; your apparel most likely has a tag that says Made In _____ (place any number of countries other than the USA; e.g., Pakistan, Mexico, Vietnam, Indonesia, China, etc.). Toys, knick-knacks, coffee mugs...? You guessed correctly if you said more are produced outside of the U.S.

The reality is that there are just fewer opportunities available today in historically well-paying blue collar industries, and many technical/professional jobs are becoming more easily outsourced to numerous countries thanks to advanced communications systems that can transport digits cheaply and quickly. (Please don't attack the internet as the problem and push policymakers to regulate intercontinental digits used in businesses that reduce a need for your skill set; rather, improve/change your skill set to be competitive in today's global economy.)

It is imperative that you realize the competitive landscape as you begin your career. Safe, long-term employment is less a reality today than in previous generations. The world is very much different, and the era of globalization in the Information Age is just getting started–we can only speculate on the impacts these drastic changes will have on society over the next 30–50 years. Therefore, it would behoove you to work to understand this dynamic, stay abreast of it, and realize continuing education is very important as you proceed. Getting a diploma or degree is a great achievement, but it is really just a starting point; it is not the end game. Update and expand your skills as often as possible. One of the biggest dislocations we have today is the masses of people who are all competing for jobs that will leave our shores (if they haven't already) and will never come back.....the old skill sets and dying industries are history, or at best living on borrowed time (think buggy whip, 8-tracks, cassettes and textbooks).

Summary – The world is a vastly different place than when your parents grew up. Globalization and the technology revolution are real, and while leveraging such is quite useful for students (cheap new gadgets, gizmos, web services, gaming platforms, etc.), the reality hits when you can't get a job in your chosen field. Or, you do get a job and find in a few years you are training your replacement in a foreign country, a replacement who has a graduate degree, five more years of experience, and requires only 1/3 the cost. Continuing education will benefit some more than others, but it is safe to say that you will likely be better off professionally if you continually update your skill set. Global competition is real, and quite fierce. Pursue professional development strategically.

2.4: 21st Century Education – Leverage the plethora of available opportunities so your dreams and passions are fulfilled according to your expectations, requirements, and living standards.

I love young idealists. They are vibrant, excited, and energetic. Eternal pessimists are negative bores in comparison. Life's too short to spend time in the doldrums with negative people, therefore, don't. Take advantage of the opportunities before your generation. The 21st century holds tremendous opportunities for those willing to work hard. Determine what you want to do and plan for success. However, in the pursuit of your passion don't lose sight of reality. Contrary to those dream-stealers who hide behind the false claim of being "realists" and use it as their default excuse, you can be a visionary, one who sees what can be, and still have a strong grasp on reality. Be careful though that you don't use following your passion as an excuse to be irresponsible. Pursue your dreams, just don't throw all caution to the wind when it comes to personal financial planning.

A common phrase exclaimed by idealists is, "but that is my passion." Great! If you can pursue your passion and meet a certain standard of living you either expect or have already begun creating, you should do it. You would be crazy not to. Though, if you cannot, and here is where actual "reality" should be applied liberally on eager young souls, you have one of two options; 1) reevaluate your desires (e.g., maybe teach high school literature until your poetry career can sail on its own), or 2) make sure your standard of living is aligned with the resources your passion can provide (ratchet down expenses).

Money won't make you happy for sure, but you do need to make a living (hint: practicality isn't altogether a bad thing); you will need to live within your means. It is not necessary to be a cardiologist at the Cleveland Clinic or a database architect at Google to have a high quality of life. You may very well be much more fulfilled by creating modern art or writing romantic poetry – honorable vocations for sure.

Follow those passions, just don't get yourself into a financial bind by trying to live a lifestyle that is larger than your current earnings.

If you can meet your standard of living by doing what you really want to do, no doubt you will be fulfilled. Be realistic about what you want out of life, and then commit to it. Life is very short and precious. Make it as enjoyable and peaceful as possible. Just don't shirk your responsibilities as you pursue your dreams (selfishness is not an honorable character trait); it is quite possible to be responsible while working toward your life goals – sacrifice will probably be necessary and usually is for most worthwhile objectives.

How does "21st Century Education" fit into this discussion? Great question. It is important to understand the massive (humongous, gargantuan, other extremely big adjectives) disruption the internet has caused over the last 20 years. Business models have been changed forever. Production, distribution channels, digital marketing, delivery... – the game has changed dramatically. All you need to do is look at the divergent outcomes of two companies, Amazon and Borders. In your lifetime Amazon was conceived and became an $87 billion leader in internet retailing, and Borders went from being the second-largest bookstore chain in the country to bankruptcy. That is only one example, and I could list a thousand more (Alibaba, Ebay, Google, WebMD, Priceline, Expedia, Salesforece.com, Facebook, Apple, etc.).

Every industry has been impacted by the internet age. However, one industry has been slow to adopt a new business model – education. But, that is changing rapidly (see K12 Learning); it has to change because, like other industries, the economics require it, and the customer is demanding it. You are a first generation digital native. That is of immense importance. You can learn anything at anytime from almost anywhere and do so very cheaply. Every generation from this point forward will expect that type of flexibility. Do you need to sit in a classroom with 30 other students and learn marketing strategies over a 16 week period from a college professor who really doesn't have any practical experience? Maybe. Or, maybe, you could go online and read blogs, articles, and e-books by current expert practitioners, and join digital marketing forums and groups (of 00s or 000s) where you can "study" at your own pace, ask questions and receive instant responses from those making hay in the marketplace today – this method may be sufficient for your needs.

Disruptive Example: Twenty years ago if you wanted to look up information on a publicly-traded company/stock you had to subscribe to an information provider who would mail a weekly or monthly periodical, or you would go to the local university library and pick up back issues of, say, Value Line (or have a broker mail his company's proprietary research). It was a slow and time-consuming process. Additionally, to buy 1,000 shares of a $25 stock from a retail broker may cost you $500, and you would have to call the order in by phone – slow, time-consuming, and expensive! – which would then be relayed to a broker in New York who would then push the order to a trader who would then execute the trade on the floor of an exchange (confirmation would follow the same route back).

Today, a junior high kid can search online and get free information on that same publicly-traded company from multiple resources, read commentary by seasoned pros, follow discussions on forums specifically dedicated to discussingthatparticularstock,doitallalmostinstantaneously, and then make an online trade in his UTMA account for $5, as he watches the depth of Level II quotes stream down his $500 laptop (which is multiples more powerful than the computers used to put the first man on the moon). It is crazy.....in one generation the costs have dropped 99% and the efficiency has increased proportionally. Talk about disruption! Talk about optimization of information!

You can learn a lot about a lot of things pretty easily by the same optimization of information effect. Let's visit an idealistic poet to create a fictional but realistic example. She is a young lady of 23, newly graduated and very passionate about becoming a successful poet. Unfortunately there are no ads in the classifieds requesting newly-minted poets, and she does need to eat and provide herself shelter, along with starting an emergency savings fund, a retirement fund, and purchasing transportation and insurance. While poet openings are scarce there is a job for a literature teacher at the local high school due to a recent retirement.

Responsibly, our young poet chooses to take a job that aligns somewhat with her education and interest, and it pays enough for her to meet her financial goals. She can now focus on her writing in the evenings after her class planning and grading is completed (she must sacrifice her free time to achieve her goal; better to do it this way than by not taking a job, not earning an income and having substantial time to write poetry though no money to buy paper to write it on). How can she leverage 21st century technologies and education to accelerate her dreams of becoming a financially independent poet?

First, she can submit her work to <u>groups and forums</u> and get vital input from a great cross section of people interested in her work, interested enough to read it and provide feedback. Without the internet, this would be nearly impossible. Today, it is easily doable, cheaply and efficiently, from her home computer. She can contact other poets, professional reviewers and college professors all over the world requesting input on her work. This is invaluable information. Once she has received input from all of these different resources she can internalize and learn from it. If she needs to improve her metaphorical usage, I am sure she can find short courses or independent programs that do such things. After honing her skills, let's assume she is ready to present her work to a broad audience. Twenty years ago she would have been unlikely to get much of an audience. Today, she can use a number of different social media platforms to post her work and ask her internet community to give her feedback. She can post her work on her own web site and drive traffic to it through search optimization and, again, leveraging her social networks.

Maybe she doesn't know anything about creating web sites or digital lead generation. Would you believe it...she can learn both skills online via blogs, groups, forums, short courses, and/or independent programs. Amazingly, via 21st century disintermediation (cutting out the middle man), she can, from her own home mind you, <u>create and publish her own poetry book</u>. She can sell it on <u>her own web site</u> with an easily-plugged in check-out cart, and/or she can sell it through any number of online distribution outlets. Instead of spending a lot of money printing hard copy books and selling them locally out of the trunk of her car, maybe reaching a hundred people, maybe a thousand, she can sell them to an online global marketplace directly from her computer via an automated delivery, check-out, and follow-up (email) service.

So you see, the 21st century digital native has a tremendous opportunity to do what those 25 years ago couldn't even dream about. You can learn everything you need to know (formally and informally) from multiple global online resources right from your home, as quickly as you are capable of learning. Then, very cheaply and effectively, as an example, you can create, <u>publish and distribute a book</u>, and collect payment (<u>PayPal</u>), not to mention provide customer service, customer surveys (<u>Survey Monkey</u>), and capture customer data, without ever leaving your house. If it works well, great, you have taken your first step to becoming a digital <u>Edgar Allan Poe</u> or Tom Clancy; if not, you are not out a lot of money relative to what it would have cost you just a generation ago, and you can decide to pivot in a different direction very quickly, say, selling homemade

Indian artwork (yes, your own online art gallery). The cost of trial and error is low, meaning you can throw a lot of mud on the wall and see what sticks as you continually develop your new skill set.

Obviously one cannot be an auto mechanic online, but an enterprising mechanic could publish an online help manual and distribute it globally for peanuts. The possibilities are only limited by your creativity and ingenuity. Not that everyone should be an "internet entrepreneur". Don't miss the point – You can learn almost anything at your own pace, on your own time (asynchronously), on your budget, from almost anywhere in the world. And as a first-generation digital native you understand how best to use all of the new applications that are coming out in droves.

While I understand the definitional change of "community" at a theoretical level, I have no interest in knowing where any of my friends are eating currently or what they think about the Super Bowl half time show in 140 characters or less. Most of you, unless you were reared by parents as disinterested in personal social networks as me and my wife, flow right into the always plugged in, constant and instant communication world that is the 21st century. This is a tremendous advantage you should understand. As a caveat – because barriers to entry are very low competition for viewers, readers, customers, etc. is escalating dramatically; you can't put up a web site and provide a product or service of little value and expect to be successful, but those who create valuable content and get it in front of a target market can be more successful more quickly than at anytime in history. That is a fact, a fact which should energize young and industrious graduates.

Simply, leverage the digital world in which you live. These are some of the most exciting times in history. From biotechnology, to new media, to international business, to educational technology, etc., opportunities abound. As one who is absolutely happy with 20th century technologies and could live peacefully without ever having heard of a smart phone, I appreciate the unique ingenuity of mankind and look forward to continual breakthroughs in medical science, advanced materials, information technologies, et al. An educated citizen will understand history, but without the wherewithal to apply this understanding in the modern world, any chance at having an impact or influence fades away as time is not spent in a productive capacity but rather in a state of nostalgia. Embrace the future; your future is now!

Summary – Follow your passion, just make sure you live within your means and budget accordingly. Some of you will make a fortune, one of you may hit the Lotto, all of you can be financially independent; whatever the case, live a fulfilling life. Money doesn't come close to buying happiness, but it does pay the bills and provide certain opportunities – use it as a means to an end, not an end.

Education, in one or more forms, is very much an input into your personal finance equation, as your ability to earn a living will directly impact your budget. 21st century "education" is efficient, effective, and on-demand; utilize it to its fullest.

Embrace the 21st century with enthusiasm – opportunities are everywhere!

DISCUSSION 3: BUDGETING AND SAVINGS

The cornerstone to your financial plan

A budget is the single most important item to personal finance success - Bar None!

<u>3.1: Create a Budget – Spend less than you earn.</u>

Two main ways to use a budget - project inflows/outflows which determine surpluses or deficits, and reconcile projected revenues (inflows) and expenses (outflows) to your actual numbers which provide the variance (difference between projected and actual budget numbers) that can be used to assess and evaluate your budgeting process and to project future budgets more accurately.

The motto of budgeting is "Do not spend more money than you earn." A novel idea for some, for others a revelation, but for the astute financial manager it is a discipline. Its corollary is "It doesn't matter how much you make, what matters is how much you keep." This is absolutely true. There are professionals who have tremendous "cash flow", but they spend every bit of it plus some (taking on more and more debt). How do you think professional athletes who make millions of dollars go bankrupt? They violate basic principles of personal finance; they don't adhere to the motto of budgeting or its corollary. Budgeting isn't difficult, though it does take a little time, a little planning, and a little (sometimes a lot of) discipline. Budget surpluses are essential to long-term wealth creation while budget deficits are destructive to your financial future.

Say you earn an average of $30,000 per year ($15/hour) over your working life; if you budget wisely, keeping your expenses lower than your earnings, and you invest a certain amount religiously, it is possible you can end up with a substantial amount of wealth at retirement. As you will learn in the next discussion, time is your very best friend when it comes to compound interest. Start early and invest every single month, and you at least put yourself in position to build up a nice retirement nest egg. It takes determination – the discipline of delayed gratification should trump the undisciplined act of immediate consumption. And it all starts with your budget, as you need surplus funds to save and invest.

Please go to Appendix B to view an actual budget. If you haven't ever done so, use a basic spreadsheet to create your personal budget projections. (If you are less comfortable with a software application, use a piece of paper and pencil.) Either create a budget right now or at least begin the process prior to January 1st of next year so you can make a New Year's Resolution to become financially independent starting with a well-planned, disciplined budget. It's not like you need to make it an official resolution or a formal procedure, but there is something to having a written document (in this case, the budget) with a signature and a date affixed. This "formality" makes things slightly more official, a touch more serious. "Ceremoniously" or not, I encourage you to print off the budget, sign and date it, and make a commitment to yourself to follow through. Your financial future is at stake, so it is a pretty important event in your life. Go ahead and get started.

Prepare next year's budget in December of the current year. Use your previous history (revenues and expenses) and any known additions/deletions to the estimated budget in your preparations. Past expense records (credit card and checking account statements), will provide a history to use to more accurately create your projected budget. Peak electric use, quarterly/annual insurance premiums, Christmas expenditures, etc. usually cause a spike in spending in certain months. As you become more cognizant of these trends, you will become better at projecting the following year's budget.

Summary - Many people get "blindsided" by spending spikes and emergency expenditures because they have never kept a personal budget – Don't get caught off guard! Prepare a budget and commit to following it on a daily, monthly, annual basis. And.....

Do NOT spend more money than you earn!

3.2: Monitor the Budget – It is a systematic, management process.

Things that cannot be measured cannot be managed. Similarly, things that are not measured are not managed. A budget can and should be measured monthly; invest the time necessary to stay on top of your finances. You should want to be a good financial manager – It's important to your future.

Everyone has their own management system, and yours may not be as useful for someone else. The key is to figure out what works best for you and follow through every month. Some people plug everything into a computer and are zealous about keeping good records and recording everything in real time. Others throw each record in a shoe box and take the last day of the month to retrieve and record everything. Then others segregate funds (for each monthly expense) at the beginning of the month and when the money is gone it is just gone (surpluses and unexpected/ emergency expenses, if any, are recorded at month end). It really doesn't matter how you do it – manual, digital, month-end, beginning of the month, meticulous, haphazard, etc. – what matters is that you DO IT!

Figure out your own system. Just remember, budgeting should not be approached as many people approach most New Year's resolutions. You don't want to stay disciplined for a month or two only to ease your way back into a comfortable, undisciplined routine. It is all about creating positive habits. Get into the habit of being financially disciplined, and before long it will be a part of your normal process. Of course this goes for eating habits, work habits, wellness habits, etc. Be disciplined and stay focused. Otherwise, you will have to live with less than optimal outcomes. There really is no need to be lazy, especially when it concerns your financial future.

Summary – Things that cannot be measured cannot be managed. Develop a management system that works for you. Be disciplined, and just Do IT!

3.3: Credit and Debt – Finance appreciating assets not depreciating assets.

It is easy to say "never go into debt" and "never use a credit card." Neither is bad advice for sure. However, most people will go into debt, and most people will use credit cards. Ideally, if you can stay out of debt and pay cash for everything you should. Realistically, you will probably not follow these principles; you have probably already violated them. So, let's try and give you secondary principles that may be almost as helpful, and possibly more applicable for a larger population.

If you are going to go into debt, make sure you can easily cover the debt payments many times over, and only finance appreciating assets. Remember that even some appreciating assets can be less than optimum investments when the interest cost combined with general inflation outpace the asset's appreciation. Plus, those interest payments may serve you better by going into an investment which will earn a return; paying someone else interest only makes the creditor wealthy.

As an example, financing a new car purchase is a bad idea. (We will assume that it is not a classic car being bought as an investment.) You are going to pay 5%-20% in interest (depending on your credit quality) and the car is going to depreciate on average 10% every year. "Losing" 15%+ per year (5% interest + 10% depreciation) is not a good financial strategy. Instead, segregate some of your savings each month to go towards a car purchase. Once you have built up enough money in your "new car savings account" to pay cash you are ready to make that purchase. Until then, it is almost always better to keep your old beater running.

If you are willing to put a little leg work into it, you can find really nice cars at great prices. And most of the time you can find better deals on used cars. Every day people turn in cars, try to sell them, or have them repossessed because they couldn't make the payments. The bank doesn't want the car returned, and the car lot will pay, at most, trade-in value, so your entry price can be substantially below retail if you are willing to do some research and negotiate. And, the lower the price the less depreciation will affect your personal balance sheet.

Buying a home is an historical example of purchasing an appreciating asset. However, after the most recent housing crash, many people would say this is a suspect notion at best. Unfortunately, in some areas homebuyers got caught up in a real estate bubble. It was a classic bubble that popped and some people will never recoup their investment. That does not change the principle. You should learn from other people's mistakes and don't repeat them. Don't be the last buyer when a "greater fool game" is being played. If you are going to play make sure you sell to a "greater fool." Otherwise, don't play in the game. With that said, most homes bought 30 years ago are worth more now than when they were originally purchased. Most bought between 2000 and 2010 will be worth more in 2040 than the original purchase price. It is a long-term investment. Even with the most recent housing malaise noted, home values in America usually appreciate over one's lifetime. (The U.S. economy and population continue to grow, however slowly, and the growth is projected to continue. Both are factors in general house price appreciation.)

As a matter of fact, you will be able to benefit from the excesses of the last real estate cycle. You will still need to be very selective with regard to price, location, growth prospects, regulation, etc. But, you should be able to find a decent house at a very good price that over the next 10-20 years should likely maintain its value or appreciate nicely barring a major exogenous event - a debt or monetary crisis or some regional/global long-term depression. (Things can and do change, sometimes quickly; and, there are no guarantees of any outcomes in this life.) A home is not usually considered only an investment though; there are other factors that make home ownership a unique concept – community, property ownership, family, work, schools. We will discuss home ownership in more detail in Discussion 5.

Credit cards are great for convenience. They are accepted almost everywhere, and some providers make it easy to itemize expenses as they do a lot of it automatically and provide a final report each month/year. It is vital to use them wisely though. How silly is it to pay interest on a hamburger and fries? Unfortunately, many people, especially many young adults keep a running balance on their credit cards. They pay 23.99% each year on a balance that was built up by purchasing clothes, food, and vacation packages. Using debt to purchase depreciating assets is bad enough, but to pay interest on consumable items---crazy! You can usually resale a car for some salvage value; however, clothes are likely sold in a garage sale for $1, and then the buyer usually haggles over that price. NEVER pay interest on perishable items, items that have no salvage value, i.e., food, clothes, vacations! It is a major financial mistake.

Pay off your credit cards each month. If plastic is going to be used, it may be just as convenient and it is more prudent to use your debit card (make sure and keep good records). Having a line of credit available for emergencies is a good idea, but using a credit card for monthly expenses (or one-time expenses like a vacation) and not paying off the balance each month is a bad idea. So, make sure and set out a sound budget at the beginning of the year, follow it diligently, and if you are going to use a credit card for convenience, make sure and pay off the balance each month.

There are times when an actual emergency expense will exceed your projected (budgeted) emergency expenses, and you may not have enough set aside to pay it all at once. This could be considered an appropriate time to use your available credit. Just make sure you alter your budget so that you can pay the balance as soon as possible. Paying 23.99% in interest is something you want to eliminate as soon as possible. All you are doing at that point is transferring your retirement funds to the bank's CEO bonus and/or retirement fund. This is a winning financial strategy, but only for the CEO; it is a losing financial strategy for you.

Summary - PAY OFF YOUR CREDIT CARD BALANCES AT THE BEGINNING OF EVERY MONTH, OR AT LEAST AS SOON AS POSSIBLE! NEVER FINANCE DEPRECIATING ASSETS AND NEVER, EVER FINANCE CONSUMABLES/CLOTHES PURCHASES.

3.4: Reserve Savings Account – Absolutely a necessity.

You should build up a reserve savings account as soon as possible. This reserve account is your buffer against potential hiccups in your revenue stream. You may change jobs and not have a regular paycheck for some time. Without a reserve savings account, a reserve fund if you will, you can really be put in a bind. Also, this reserve fund can be regarded as a back-up emergency fund. When something unanticipated comes up that exceeds your budgeted emergency expenses, you can use the reserve fund as an emergency back up instead of a credit card (per the scenario above), possibly saving you substantial interest costs.

Personal finance experts believe a reserve fund should have enough in it to cover three months, six months, and even twelve months of budgeted expenses. In reality, the more the better! Three months would be a good starting point. Do your best to get the reserve fund up to at least twelve months of expenses. And any time you dip into it, make sure and build it back up as soon as possible. Having a properly funded reserve savings account is absolutely essential to prudent personal finance. Make a serious effort to build up this fund as soon as possible and be disciplined not to dip into it for frivolous purchases just because it is a big chunk of cash sitting there - It serves a valuable purpose and should be treated as such.

Summary – This is not a slush fund; use it as a reserve fund and a back-up emergency fund. Build it up as quickly as possible. I assure you, discipline in building and managing the reserve fund will pay off in spades at a time when you really need it.

3.5: Long-term Savings – Building the liquid portion of long-term, conservative assets on your balance sheet.

Over time it is very likely that your overall investment portfolio will consist of a few investment vehicles; IRA, 401k, annuities, etc. Each will probably be made up of multiple asset classes. (In the next discussion we address Portfolio Management and Diversification). It would be prudent to have a certain amount of cash (conservative, liquid – immediately available) included in the mix.

Of course you will have conservative, liquid investments in your emergency fund and reserve fund, but you want to account for those monies separately. Those funds have distinct and independent purposes (emergency; unexpected disruptions to earnings and back-up emergency). A long-term savings account should be looked at more like a very safe asset in the investment mix that does two things; 1) it provides stability to your other investments which will likely fluctuate due to market volatility, and, 2) it provides liquid assets to take advantage of opportunities that arise unexpectedly so you can make quick investments without selling other assets that have early withdraw penalties, tax consequences, or are illiquid. The size of this account will grow as your larger long-term investment portfolio grows.

There is never anything wrong with having cash around. Some will tell you that you need to have your money working for you. That is true, but "cash as king" is true as well. Even in low interest rate and high-inflation environments there will be opportunities that arise and require cash-on-hand to close a deal. Each situation is different due to multiple factors, but rarely has anyone ever gone bankrupt by having too much cash on his balance sheet!

Summary – Savings accounts are conservative (guaranteed by the US Government up to a certain amount) which mollify your total risk profile and provide easily-accessible liquid assets when necessary. And, rarely has anyone ever gone bankrupt by having too much cash.

DISCUSSION 4: INVESTING

The idea that money should work for you

4.1: Investing Terminology – There is industry terminology and jargon in every field, and gaining a working base of knowledge is helpful for improved understanding.

For an Extended List of Helpful Investment Terms – See "Glossary" at the end of the book.

Professional investing/finance has its own language – convexity, quick ratio, stochastics, Sharpe ratio, CAPM, etc. – just as most any other profession:

> Football Coach – Liz pro wide, zip, 28 quick pitch crack, on two…

> Medical Doctor – A slight strain in the medial head of the gastrocnemius caused by a sudden extension of the knee with the foot in dorsiflexion.

To invest one doesn't need to know all of the language of the professional investment community, but it does help to discern information if you understand industry jargon. Increasing fluency will be a responsibility you need to handle mostly on your own based upon your interest and acumen. For our purposes we will only use language necessary to meet the needs of this primer. While it is helpful to speak the lingo, it is not necessary to do so to make an investment.

Mutual Fund is a term with which you should become very familiar. A mutual fund is a vehicle that allows investors, especially those just starting out, to hire professional money managers cheaply and efficiently. Mutual funds also help investors with fewer resources to diversify an investment portfolio. These benefits make mutual funds appropriate investment vehicles for most anybody, but especially for new investors.

What, exactly, is a mutual fund? If you read through a prospectus, which by federal regulation you are required to receive, the *legalese* – wording and structure - is very dry, and many consider that characterization rather generous. In theory the mandate to provide a prospectus is reasonable, in practice very few investors ever read through the document. Drafting and distribution costs are much higher than value received per individual investor, but I suspect a majority of well-intentioned legislation could be described similarly. With that said, after separating the legal filler from the helpful parts of the document, the prospectus does provide some useful information – management fees, expenses, 12b-1 fees, management team information, fund parameters, past performance, etc. (Usually most of this information is readily available in easily-accessible format via fund company web sites.) Anyway, take a little time and read a prospectus or two or three and you will quickly be able to discern those sections which are applicable and those which are better described as vanilla legal filler.

So, what is a mutual fund? Let's take each word and define it independently.

Mutual – having the same specified relationship to each other.
Fund – a supply (of money) set aside or made available for a particular purpose.

Therefore, a mutual fund, by this simplistic definitional process, should be a pool of investors (those who supply money) with pro rata interest (same specified relationship) who come together to make an investment(s) (a particular purpose). Could it be so simple? As a matter of fact it is; a mutual fund is the sum of the individual definitions.

A mutual fund is a company set up to pool individual investor funds so that professional money managers can efficiently manage the funds of those (thousands/tens of thousands) investors, all who have similar investment purposes. This type of vehicle allows smaller investors the ability to hire professional managers and diversify their holdings when otherwise they would have a hard time doing either independent of the mutual fund. Likewise, it is a very good way for investment companies to efficiently and effectively manage funds for very large numbers of investors; it is a scalable business plan and one which is highly profitable for those companies that execute well.

We will discuss portfolio management and diversification in later sections, but before we go any further I think it best to address some terms with regard to mutual funds, key terms that will help your general knowledge. Understanding terminology eliminates a lot of people's apprehensions when it comes to investing. Behind all the mystery of finance, the great wizards really are just simple, unassuming, normal people. Thankfully, investing is not mysterious and doesn't require incantations.

Here are a few "technical" terms to get you started.

* Investment Company = Sponsor of the fund, the entity which forms the mutual fund.

* Mutual Fund = The legal entity in which the investors invest; a company independent in its own right, but started and managed by an affiliated investment company.

* Investor = You and all of the other people who send a check to the Investment Company specifically earmarked for investment in a particular mutual fund.

* Net Asset Value (NAV) = NAV is the price you pay per unit to participate in the fund; it is calculated daily by dividing the total assets by total number of units issued – Total Assets / Total Units = NAV.

   (A no-load mutual fund company which has 1MM units outstanding and $10MM in cash and securities has an NAV of $10. If the next investor deposited $1MM, and all current assets remained static, the fund would issue 100,000 additional units, changing the numerator and denominator but not the NAV as you will see in the following - $11MM/1.1MM = $10;

therefore, there is no dilution when the fund takes on more money and the NAV is purely determined by a simple calculation of the cash and securities owned by the fund relative to its corresponding issued units.).

* Unit = A unit is what an investor owns in an open-end mutual fund. Contrary to popular understanding, especially for new investors, an investor does not own shares, or have ownership rights, in the individual securities the fund owns; i.e., the investor will not have a right to vote in an individual company's meetings or via proxy – a typical ownership right of a direct shareholder. The mutual fund investor votes just on those things which affect the mutual fund as this is what the investor actually owns. Therefore, the investor's interest is completely in the returns generated by the fund (financial interest) and the management of said fund (ownership interest). The mutual fund investor only has an indirect financial interest in the individual securities owned by the fund. [It is always good to understand ownership structure and the rights which accompany one's ownership/financial interest.]

* Bid/Offer = No-load mutual funds have equal bid/ offer price NAVs; Load mutual funds (those which charge a certain amount to participate: 5.75%, 3%, etc.) have a spread in the bid/offer price that corresponds to the load charged.

* No-load Funds = Mutual Funds which do not assess a sales charge for investors to invest.

*   Load Funds = Mutual Funds which assess a sales charge to participate.

*   Class A Funds = Mutual funds which have a front-end sales charge, e.g., 5% of all new money into the fund.

*   Class B Funds = Mutual funds which have a back-end sales charge, usually decreasing over time, e.g., 5% on redemptions in the first year, 4% in year two, 3% in year three, etc.

*   Class C Funds = Mutual funds which have a set annual charge as a percentage of assets, e.g., 1% per year.

*   Management Fee = Amount the fund management company receives as a percentage of assets under management, usually assessed each quarter. Note: management fee is not a charge the investor sees directly (like a front-end sales charge); the fee is 'absorbed' by the assets of the fund and shows up in annual Net Return figures.

*   Expense Fee = Amount segregated to pay for the expenses of the fund; accounting, legal, transactions, etc. Note: expense fee is handled similarly to the management fee.

*   12b-1 fees = Fees some funds charge for marketing expenses.

* Annual Returns = Annual Performance in percentage terms for a calendar year. When comparing different mutual funds' historical performance it is prudent to compare Net Returns so that all fees and charges are accounted for properly. (Annual returns are determined by changes in unrealized capital gains, realized capital gains, dividends and interest.)

It is too simplistic to say one should only invest in no-load mutual funds because there are not any sales charges. While you should take all fees into consideration, it is completely justified to pay a broker and a mutual fund company reasonable fees if they provide superior performance, customer service, education and/or other value-add services. Financial consulting is a business which requires profitability to remain viable. (A broker cannot make any money selling no-load mutual funds without charging some sort of management fee or wrap account fee. He has to pay bills like the rest of us.) However, it is sensible to state that low-cost, no-load mutual funds do have the potential to provide a higher net return over time specifically because they keep fees (which decrease returns to the investor) low.

You just have to take a little time, perform some basic research, and apply elementary mathematics to determine which type of fund works best for you. Paying little in fees to underperform your specific benchmark doesn't make much sense if by paying higher fees you could outperform the same benchmark. Your primary investment goal is not to see how few fees you can pay over an investment lifetime;

more likely, it is to generate the highest <u>net return</u> (return after all fees are assessed) possible over your investment life.

There are, both, high-quality and low-quality load funds, no-load funds, stockbrokers, financial planners, investment consultants, advisors, etc. Work with those people/firms who meet your investment return objectives, customer service expectations, and all other requirements you deem necessary. From Vanguard to 20th Century (now American Century) to Charles Schwab to Merrill Lynch to JP Morgan Securities and many, many others, it is not hard to find good people, products and services. Be diligent, though, and always remember you may be able to 'Trust Chuck' (Charles Schwab), and I believe you can, but ol' Chuck, while a great guy I am sure, will never care as much about your financial well-being as you do. And I suspect he would be the first person to confirm this idea of personal diligence (responsibility/accountability).

I started with mutual fund terminology because I believe mutual funds are great vehicles for early investors. They allow you to leverage experienced, successful, professionals as you diversify into:

> corporate and government bonds; asset-backed securities; developed/developing/emerging/frontier-country stocks and bonds; large/medium/small domestic stocks; hard assets/commodities; derivative products; etc.

That's a lot of 'stuff' to know for anybody let alone a young adult who is just starting out!

No one can be an expert in all of these different areas. A non-professional investor will have a hard time becoming an expert in large cap domestic stocks, much less all of the rest. Instead of assembling your own basket of diversified securities, go ahead and buy a few mutual funds and hire some of the best in the business to do it for you. Trying to invest $5,000 into 100 different positions (many mutual funds own 100+ securities) has net return-suppressing transaction costs. Even with technology and substantially-reduced commissions (cost of buying a stock), it really doesn't make a lot of sense for non-professional (those who are not money managers) small investors to try and manage a portfolio of numerous independent positions.

Now, there is no reason to own 100 securities per se. You can get plenty of diversification in far fewer positions. And there is nothing wrong with building your own portfolio made up of independent securities. It is actually a great way to learn the ropes. However, experience has shown that a vast majority of non-professional investors do not have the time or are not willing to spend the time to perform proper investor due diligence.

If you are going to buy a security it is important that you know its structure, the fundamentals of the company issuing the security, the economic drivers of the company, the financial drivers of the security's price, and how it fits into your overall portfolio. It's not prohibitively difficult, but it does take a significant investment of time. Too many people see investing as picking black or red at the roulette wheel. Investing does carry risk, but it is not a game of chance; it shouldn't be approached like a weekend in Vegas. If you are going to do so, it seems logical that you should probably just hire a mutual fund manager.

Think about it – 1% of $5,000 is $50. You can hire some of the best mutual fund managers/management teams in the industry for $50, <u>per year</u>! Compare that value to going on a date at a decent steakhouse or sushi bar —- there is no comparison, economically speaking.

A few more typical terms:

* Asset Allocation = To balance risk and reward by allocating/apportioning assets according to goals, risk tolerance and investment time frame; a simple asset allocation model consisting of the principle asset classes would be: 55% equities / 30% fixed income / 15% cash.

* Equity = A stock or any other security representing an ownership interest.

* Fixed Income = A security that provides a return in the form of fixed payments and an eventual return of principal at maturity; e.g., a 3%, 30-year, U.S. Treasury bond.

* Closed-end Mutual Fund = A listed and publicly-traded investment fund that raises a fixed amount of capital through an initial public offering. Shares are priced on the exchange just like any typical stock

on the secondary market and valued by supply and demand of the marketplace. Closed-end funds will usually trade at a premium or discount to the Net Asset Value of the fund (though they can trade equal to the current NAV) unlike open-end funds which trade daily at the NAV.

* ETF / ETN (Exchange Traded Fund / Exchange Traded Note) = Securities that can be simple (tracking a well-known index, S&P 500) or complex (triple shorting an index, going long a single commodity or basket of commodities, pitting one currency against another-currency cross, etc.), trade in the secondary market via an exchange (e.g., NYSE – New York Stock Exchange), and are passively 'managed'.

* Ordinary Dividends = A distribution to shareholders of a portion of a company's earnings, decided by the Board of Directors.

* Dividend Yield = A financial ratio that shows how much a company pays in dividends each year relative to its share price; Annual Dividends Per Share / Price Per Share ($3 Annual Dividend / $60 Share Price = 5% Dividend Yield).

* Interest = A non-principal payment to those who lend money. Example: Banks borrow money from depositors through savings accounts or certificates of deposit to loan out to retail borrowers or invest in securities; for access to this capital banks pay the

depositors interest on their money. Companies or governments borrow money from investors by issuing bonds; for access to this capital the company or government pays investors interest (per the payment schedule – monthly, quarterly, semi-annually, or annually) on this investment.

* Capital Gains (Realized / Unrealized) = An increase in the value of an asset/investment above its purchase price. If the asset is sold for a profit, it is considered a realized capital gain. A capital gain is either short term (one year or less) or long term (held for more than one year). If the asset is not sold but trades above its purchase price it is considered an unrealized capital gain.

* Security = A financial instrument (stocks, bonds, debentures, notes, options, futures, swaps, warrants, etc.) representing ownership (e.g., stock), a debt agreement (e.g., bond) or the rights to ownership (as a derivative).

There are numerous online resources that you can use to look up investment terms - Type "investment terminology" into your search engine.

Summary – There are a few things to learn. Thankfully, it is all fairly easy. I have met a number of football coaches in my lifetime and few of them were excessively academic or cerebral. However, if an average person listened to a high school football offensive coordinator at any typical program in the country, this person would be quite impressed because the coach really does speak a 'foreign' language, and likely speaks it fluently. This acquired skill does not indicate he is a brainiac, or a good coach for that matter, though it does show he has invested a substantial amount of time learning the lingo and playing in his sandbox. Likewise, as you spend time in the investment sandbox you will learn industry terminology and jargon. It is no harder than learning an offensive playbook. With that said it does take time and effort. No worries - you'll get it.

4.2: Investing Basics – Buy low / sell high.

I know.....great advice (buy low/sell high), really insightful. Actually, it is not meant to start a deep technical conversation, but it is much more than a cliché, and probably a bit deeper than you initially think. The reality is that professionals and non-professionals alike violate this one basic rule of investing more than you would believe. And it's not because they plan to make bad decisions, or that they do not know the rule. It is 100% because they are typically human, meaning, they are rational and emotional beings, and they aren't always right.

Let me tell you a story that underscores human nature, a fictional story for sure but one which occurs over and over, day after day, generation after generation. (Focus on the principles in the storyline and not necessarily the slightly extreme particular details.)

Mr. I.M. Money invests $10,000 in Stock A at $10 per share. Stock A goes to $11 and Mr. Money is feeling really good. He is up 10% in a month, and he is bragging to his co-workers that at this pace he will earn 120% per year. Everyone is impressed and expresses an interest in depositing money into his new hedge fund once he quits his current job. Things are going well. Mr. Money is planning office décor and couldn't be more pleased with Stock A's performance. He is really getting to like Stock A.

However, the stock begins to dip down a bit because of competition in the industry. Soon the share price is back down to $10. Mr. Money isn't worried; he knows this stock, loves this stock, and understands its business much better than Mr. Market - all other participants buying and selling the shares of Stock A. Mr. Money believes in it so much he adds another 1,000 shares at $10, even though his daughter is just about to turn 16 and is really looking forward to her first car. Mr. Money figures if he can double this *car money* he will be able to use the profits to actually get Princess a brand new first car and keep the principal working in his new hedge fund.

Unfortunately, the SEC announces they are opening an investigation into Stock A. It seems their accounting is suspect. In short order Stock A is now trading at $7 per share. Mr. Money is feeling much less confident about the company and its stock price. Yet, Mr. Money believes the

SEC will soon find that the company didn't do anything wrong and he will be back in business; this is just a minor bump in the road. Though, he is starting to lose sleep at night - nightmares that the SEC may be right. And, if they are, will it be a minor slap on the wrist or will the whole management team end up alongside Fastow, Ebbers, or Madoff? Soon, Mr. Money is beginning to wake up, that is when he can actually fall asleep, consistently each night in a cold sweat. Yes, it is only a $6,000 loss, but after Princess' used car purchase ($10,000) he will only have $4,000 left over. Better than nothing, but Mrs. Money was expecting to take the kids to Sea World this summer with the "investment" funds, and she will be more than irate if Mr. Money's "mid-life career crisis" jeopardizes family memories.

No prob, it will all work out. These things happen all the time. Mr. Money figures the weak-kneed amateurs were all selling from $10 to $7. Now that the only holders of the stock are strong hands like his, the selling pressure will subside, and when the SEC finds no wrongdoing the stock price will rebound in a big way. Except, the company just announced a big earnings miss and all the analysts are questioning the integrity of the accounting. On the most recent conference call management is short and abrasive and refuses to address any question with substance. They seem like they are hiding something. Within an hour after the conference call Stock A is trading under $5!

Mr. Money is now in a panic. The company is going under for sure. All of those guys are crooks, and the SEC can't let any more fraudsters off easily. Plus, new competition is causing a price war and these new entrants are willing to lose money to gain market share rapidly. The reasons to own this stock are down to slim and none, and slim is leaving town. And worst of all, Mr. Money can't even pay for the car he promised Princess, much less the Sea World vacation. If the stock goes to $0, Princess will not get her car, she will hate Mr. Money, and Mrs. Money is already going to blow a gasket – what would she do if Mr. Money rode this dog down to $0?

SELL, SELL!!! Mr. Money gets out of Stock A at $4.50, a 55% loss. His 2,000 shares went from a value of $20,000 to $9,000 in less than 4 months. How in the world is he going to explain this fiasco to Mrs. Money? She still thinks he is in the process of "paper trading" his new hedge fund.

At least he can sleep at night. No more cold sweats. No more worrying about SEC investigations or accounting fraud. Yeah, the co-workers are providing some ribbing, but Mr. Money postures strongly, he let's them know that real traders are always willing to take losses. That is how the pros make the big money, but none of the office grunts understand because they don't know much about real money. And for their rudeness he vows never to give them his stock advice, which could be very costly as his next pick may double in a month or two.

Mr. Money does purchase his daughter a car on her Sweet 16, though he has to borrow a thousand dollars from the bank to make up for what he lost on Stock A. He fesses up to Mrs. Money and discloses that he lost $11,000 and a trip to Sea World is not in the cards this year......or probably next, but they do get to carry the investment losses forward on their tax returns for 4 years. Of course Mrs. Money is less than thrilled with this hair-brained debacle and fumes over all the things they could have done with $11,000. Mr. Money defends himself by saying that he could have stayed in like those fools that did and lost the other $9,000 once the company declares bankruptcy. Mrs. Money should be patting him on the back for saving $9,000 instead of giving him a hard time. She doesn't see it that way and strongly demands that Mr. Money not invest another dime until he awakens from this self-delusion and puts some reasonable safe guards in place so nothing like this (or worse) ever happens again.

Kind of crazy, don't you think? It (the psychological stress, emotional roller coaster, and, very probably, the irritated spouse) happens all the time. But, there is more to this sad tale. This is where the psychological stress turns into real trauma.

The rest of the story......Stock A does rebound. It never goes below $4.50. Management seemed less than forthcoming with analysts because they had run the company they founded for 20 years with the highest integrity. They felt they had answered the questions honestly and refused to continue to defend themselves against unsubstantiated claims which were bordering on personal attacks. There was no fraud. Add to the reduced threat of an SEC investigation, the new competition started to falter because their massive losses didn't lead to increased market share. It became obvious the competition's losing business plan had a very short shelf life. Stock A renewed margin expansion as they reclaimed market share. The stock price may very well hit $15 in the same calendar year that it traded at $4.50.

Mr. Money has already done the math. If he would have stayed in the game, at $15 per share he could have sold his 2,000 shares for a $5 profit ($10,000). Mrs. Money could have had her Sea World trip, plus some extras, and just the profits would have paid for Princess's car. Mr. Money not only lost $11,000, but he is beating himself up daily for not having more courage when things were at their worst. He was right all along; he believes he very well could run a hedge fund – how many hedge funds make 50% per year like he would have in Stock A?

The reality is that Mr. Money has a long way to go before he will ever be able to make another investment. He is now emotionally whipped. He will be gun shy for a long time to come, and rightly so. He was correct in that losing money is a part of the process, but he doesn't understand risk management, money management, trade management, and/or portfolio management. Losses must be limited and manageable; they should never have the potential to wipe out your whole investment account. Gambling and investing are two totally different animals.

Mr. Money bought high and sold low; he broke the most basic of rules. Two extreme alternative endings (and innumerous in between) could have played out.

1) Mr. Money could have purchased another 1,000 shares on margin (borrowing the broker's capital) at $5 reducing his cost of ownership to $8.33 per share. He then could have sold the 3,000 shares at $15 per share and made $20,000 (after repaying the borrowed $5,000) on a $20,000 equity investment (a 100% return) in less than a year. A seasoned pro, depending on his other trading positions, might very well have implemented this strategy. Mr. Money showed that he was not a seasoned pro and should stick to his day job.

2) Mr. Money could have purchased the additional 1,000 shares at $5 as stated above. However, in this scenario, the company does go bankrupt and all common stockholders (of which Mr. Money was one of many) get wiped out. Mr. Money would have lost all of his $20,000 cash investment PLUS the $5,000 he borrowed on margin. This likely would have put Mrs. Money over the edge.

No doubt there are a lot of stories of seasoned pros (and amateurs) doing just such a thing. Being a professional trader doesn't immune one from humanity, even though some would argue that point. They are driven by greed and fear just as Mr. Money. They just have more experience in how to handle such a situation, and, hopefully, a risk management group within the firm that steps in when it is obvious all rationality has been lost.

I could point you to any number of high-profile trading debacles as case studies, situations where a trader or a firm were wiped out (MF Global comes to mind directly), but one that really intrigued me was the story of Nick Leeson. The guy single-handedly took down Barings Bank, a 200-year old British institution, the Queen's bank for goodness sakes. Can you imagine? Anyway, it is a simple storyline that is true time and again – greed and fear unchecked lead to ruin.

Yes, I will accept that "buy low / sell high" is a banal statement, but I encourage you to accept that it is also a phrase steeped in wisdom and should be a basic, fundamental investment principle. Strategically, it is really simple – no need to make things more complex than required – yet, still deep and thought provoking, and it should be engrained in practice as much as possible. In reality an investor will inevitably buy high and sell low many times. It is the nature of the business – you will suffer losses. The goal is to limit your losses, manage your risk, and do so in the context of an overall portfolio approach. If you can't help but to gamble, segregate those funds and only use a small percentage of your total assets. If you bet right, those gains can add a little juice to your returns for sure. However, if you lose the bet, this loss should never, ever, under any circumstance, jeopardize your financial well-being.

Summary – We are and always will be rational AND emotional beings. Understand that human nature does not check itself at the door when one invests – it is amplified. Greed and fear drive decisions, many times bad ones; thus, limit the extremes of your emotions when investing. (Never fall in love with a security. Think of securities as inanimate objects of utility, nothing more or less, like a pencil; use them as means to an end - your financial independence.) Embrace the simplicity and wisdom of "buy low / sell high"; use it as one of a few guiding principles to your investment strategy. And understand what it really means in a nutshell - **focus on proper investment management and overall profits**; without profitable investments you will never reach your financial goals, and any position that threatens your goals should be scrutinized greatly.

4.3: Introduction to Portfolio Management – Keep It Simple Sweetheart.

The KISS acronym is popular in many circles for obvious reasons (simplicity is understandable, transferable & efficient, and it works). For our purposes we really want to reduce any financial complexity to a few basic principles. Portfolio management is actually one of those disciplines that can lose people because of the math. We won't go there in any depth. It's not necessary, but if you want to dig a little deeper into placing investments on the efficient frontier curve pick up any college text on Portfolio Management / Modern Portfolio Theory. It will have all you need (SML, CAPM, covariance, standard deviation...) to keep you busy for a while. Nothing I believe you couldn't handle, but it is out of our scope.

In this section we will discuss just a few concepts; 'know thyself', asset allocation, diversification, and risk management. My goal is to provide a foundation that gives you all you need to get started and gives you something from which you can build upon if you so choose. I can't tell you what to invest in specifically as that is a much more individualized process, but if you invest within the framework presented in this section, I think you will be well ahead of a significant portion of the population at large, and possibly ahead of a majority of the investing population. Unfortunately, that is not hyperbole, it is the sad truth.

Know Thyself

This knowledge is derived from a personal inventory which every investor should take. You need to define who you are as an investor, what you want out of your investments, and how your current financial picture can support an investment campaign. There are four main items you should define clearly in terms of how they apply to you personally before managing (even overseeing management of) your investment portfolio: 1) risk aversion; 2) time frame; 3) objectives; and 4) cash flow. It is paramount to "Know Thyself" when investing real dollars to meet important financial goals.

Risk Aversion

Risk aversion can be a tricky item to measure. It is very fluid to say the least. To be risk averse just means to avoid risk. Highly risk-averse people will never take any risk regardless of the potential returns. They can't stomach the thought of losing what they have. Seriously, it makes them ill; they can't eat or sleep. This level of aversion is obviously unhealthy in most circumstances, but it is a reality and should be understood as such. It would be very hard to be highly risk averse and an investor of any kind (maybe a community banker, but not an investor).

I don't think a study has been done, but I suspect if you were to poll a decent sampling of average investors most would say they are conservative growth investors. Some would be aggressive and a few would be very conservative, though most would fall within a fairly predictable range around "conservative growth." However, attitudes change when volatility spikes and losses come fast and furious; once it happens a large portion of this group will come to realize they really don't want the risk involved with growth investing. And we are not talking about maneuvering a portfolio to defend against downside risks. We are talking about investors who seem to have a fundamental change in their core personalities. Now, they really don't change, they just realize through external pressure that they mischaracterized their level of risk aversion. This is very typical. By knowing yourself through honest assessment, you won't have to "change" when the markets move against some of your investments. If you are losing a lot of sleep at night when "corrections" occur, you may have been too aggressive in your personal inventory. Losing some sleep is probably natural, losing a lot of sleep isn't a healthy long-term proposition.

On the other hand, there are those who may think they are fairly conservative only to find out that when losses and high volatility hit they really don't weigh on them as risk is accepted as a natural order of things, i.e., potential higher rewards are met with corresponding risk and potential losses. This personality/attitude can (not should necessarily, but can) likely accept more risk than originally thought and much more than the highly risk-averse individual.

Risk tolerance levels aren't easy to nail down, but there are numerous risk tolerance tests you can find online that can assist you in determining a base line. (Type "risk tolerance quiz" into your search engine and pick from a plethora of options.)

Understand that residing on one end of the risk aversion line is not better or worse than being on the other end (risk taker [comfortable with risk]-----risk avoider [uncomfortable with risk]); it just is what it is. Either way, risk aversion assessment is but one input into your personal inventory. If you are accurate about who you are as a person you will be a much better investor because your investment portfolio will closely match your individual make up, or at least it should.

Your goal is to use your cash/cash flow to develop a portfolio that corresponds to your <u>risk</u> <u>appetite</u> and will meet your investment objectives over a specified time frame - It's not any more complex than that.

Time Frame

What is your time frame? As a young adult, we can assume that your retirement portfolio is a long-term proposition. At your age time is a huge asset. You have time to earn back losses and see gains compound. Those in or near retirement do not have that luxury – time for these folks has become more of a liability; at best, time cannot be leveraged to build wealth with this shorter time horizon nor to meet quite different, usually, objectives. If you were to quantify your time horizon for retirement, you would place it at 10 (on a scale of 1-10, with 10 indicating that time can be used as an asset and 1 indicating that time is now a definite liability in meeting long-term goals).

Objectives

Of course, you have many goals for which you invest; down payment for a home, new car, wedding/honeymoon, etc. These usually have shorter-term investment horizons than retirement and would tend to move these types of investments more toward the middle or other end of the time-frame scale (above), depending on when the cash is actually needed. Without getting into the weeds too much, as you build your investment portfolio you will actually be building multiple "mini-portfolios" that are designed to meet certain objectives, and in this process you will have developed a sort of meta-portfolio, if you will. This is really only a natural outgrowth and not a purposeful design, but it will be interesting to compile once you have all of your particular portfolios structured.

Cash Flow

Nothing can be commenced until you have available funds, which is why your budget is of primary importance. If you have a large, lump-sum of cash handy, you will be less prohibited than the average young adult/graduate with regard to funding your investment portfolios. Initially, a majority of graduates will only have cash flow from which to invest. That is why it is so important to have a budget surplus – you earn more than you spend - at the end of each month. Otherwise, you will never (outside of a Lotto win or other random fortune) get ahead. Unfortunately, there is no way to work around the basic tenet of surplus cash flow; you either earn enough to cover your personal expenses AND to invest, or you don't. If you don't have a surplus you can do one of three things – increase your earnings, reduce your expenses, or (preferably) both. It may sound unsympathetic, but it's just life. Inconveniently, life isn't that easy, and it can be utterly difficult at times.

You can make "Know Thyself" an art form or you can operate mechanically. As an art form, ask yourself sensible questions, questions you deem pertinent to a self evaluation, answer them honestly, and create/manage your portfolios according to your qualitative assessment. As in most art this process is highly arbitrary. If you can handle the innate subjectivity and work well under this system, by all means follow what works for you. If you need something a bit more quantifiable, use a numbering system. Give all 4 items (risk aversion, time frame, objectives, cash flow) a 1-10 scale; weigh each item equally, or apply independent weighting to each based upon your own methodology (for our purposes we will stick with a basic equal-weight scale, but as you develop a customized system for yourself you may want to add more items and/or varied weighting schemes). Following is an example:

Equal Weight -
Scale: 1-10

Risk = 5 (lower number equals "more risk averse")
Time Frame = 5 (lower number equals "less time on your side")
Objectives = 5 (lower number equals "important not to lose money")
Cash Flow = 1 (lower number equals "less available funds")
Total = 16

What does 16 mean? If the total value of points possible is 40, as it is here, you may set up a model that says something like this –

1-4 =	Totally Risk Averse (Only put the money under your mattress)
5-10 =	Very Conservative
11-20 =	Moderately Conservative
21-30 =	Conservative Growth
31-35 =	Aggressive
36-40 =	Very Aggressive

The model is not etched in stone because it is flexible as you are at liberty to weight items according to your unique situation. Of course you should have reasonable ranges that make application fruitful. Use the above system until you develop a personal model that works best for you, and apply the system to each of your portfolios.

It is very important to Know Thyself. An honest personal inventory is foundational to personal portfolio management.

We still have a loose end to address to complete the process. The example inventory puts one in the moderately conservative (Score = 16) camp. So.....what does that mean with regard to an actual portfolio?

As we move into asset allocation and diversification we will address this loose end. Do not expect finite answers though. Investing is somewhat akin to economics, and, as is often quipped, there is nothing worse than a two-handed economist, other than an economist with more than two hands.

I will try to reduce the complexity to some simple, basic principles, and in doing so many experts will contend that the discussion is not complete. I am not going to argue that point, but I will say that that is OK.

My goal is not to develop expert financial theorists or polemicists who will defend my view of the value of simplicity in this short book. My goal is to provide each reader a solid framework from which one can start a personal finance journey with some knowledge, a little confidence, and a foundation that can be built upon.

Asset Allocation

Asset allocation is as simple as it sounds – it just means using your cash (one asset) to buy a number of other (process of allocation) securities in multiple asset classes (stocks, bonds, real estate, commodities…). For example if you have $1,000 in your savings account and you decide to buy units in a domestic small cap stock mutual fund equal to $250, an investment grade corporate bond mutual fund equal to $250, an international large cap mutual fund equal to $250, and purchase shares in a gold ETF equal to $250, you have just allocated assets and created an investment portfolio.

That's it? Yes, that is about all there is to it. We can make it a lot more sophisticated (adding asset classes that are made up of securities that few people understand well – Credit Default Swaps, as an example), but once you get the gist of the process you can pretty much expand it as necessary to meet your needs. The average retail investor doesn't do much CDS business or derivative-type business (options, P/Os, I/Os, options on futures, etc.). It's not necessary to understand intimately every product Wall Street financial engineers create. You can construct a well-balanced portfolio with your more typical asset classes and do just fine over your investment lifetime. Some of you may want to deep dive into financial industry minutia, and even create your own derivative of a derivative-type product one day. I wouldn't discourage it; you can do quite well in finance if you have a quantitative acumen. Nonetheless, the rest of us will become physical therapists or school counselors, coach little league baseball, and invest in things we understand (most everyone gets how Wal-Mart makes money), or hire mutual fund managers to do it for us.

Basic asset allocation provides a certain level of diversification; however, we will use the concept of diversification within asset classes to reduce unsystematic risk. (More on that in a bit.) Understanding the process of asset allocation is important, but by itself it doesn't necessarily help one create a personal portfolio that addresses specific goals. So, we need to go one step further in our discussion.

A few points before we proceed on asset allocation. I think now is the time to make crystal clear that investing is highly individualized. Sure, two 21-year olds with similar cash flows investing for retirement will likely have more in common with each other than either will have with a typical octogenarian, but that doesn't mean one can mirror the other's retirement investment portfolio. People have very different appetites for risk, different goals, different lifestyles, and different values. You must be 100% comfortable with your decision-making process, not half-hearted about someone else's.

When volatility comes and certain positions become losses (both will happen over time) you will need faith in the investment plan you prepared to withstand these difficult times. If you don't know why you own something or you do not have confidence in the plan, you will very easily make emotional decisions. Emotional decisions are natural, and sometimes emotional decisions are reasonable; yet, many times strong emotions lead to irrational decisions, and they almost always trump reason in times of stress, unless you have properly prepared for adversity. People don't plan to fail, they fail to plan. But, if you use someone else's plan, you very well may fail anyway.

By reading this book you have made a mature decision. Continue to invest some of your time applying what you learn and growing as an investor. Along with 4t Nox U, there are many other resources available to assist you in developing a personal investment plan. Be proactive in your continuing education. I promise it will pay dividends in the long term.

Back to proper asset allocation. The goal of asset allocation is to give you exposure to multiple asset classes on the idea that not every asset class goes up and down together. Sometimes bonds go up when stocks go down, and vice versa. Other times commodities go up when the value of the dollar goes down due to monetary inflation. Obviously if someone had figured out a 100% correlation in asset classes (stocks go up 10% every time bonds go down 10%) investing would be much easier. The reality is that because of so many dynamic factors in the marketplace it is impossible to ever be sure of any long-term direct correlations. One thing you can say with complete confidence is that when the stock market goes up 10% the stock market went up 10%. It would be next to impossible to make any finite claims about other asset classes because of the 10% stock market gain or to make an accurate prognostication of the next stock market move, up or down. Rarely, if ever, does one asset class coincide with another consistently over time at the same ratio. And candidly, causation would be more helpful if we were looking to maximize gains, but that is really a tough game to play without 20/20 hindsight. Now, there are seasonal factors, and there are strong correlations in certain time periods, but none of that is iron clad. Things change – choppy markets begin to trend; trends settle into choppy markets; correlations appear, disappear, and reappear; causes become effects.....the market is very dynamic (which by the way is really cool).

Getting any advantage (seasonal factors, correlations, etc.) you can makes sense, but now we are getting down into the weeds pretty deeply. Again, I wouldn't discourage anyone from doing so because hard work can produce substantial rewards. It's just getting away from our focus on basics.

Asset allocation will not insure you against a wholesale sell-off like we saw in 2008-2009 (many bonds got hammered, especially lower quality bonds, stocks were crushed all over the world, commodities were in free fall.....it was a mess), but it can soften the blow to your portfolio. Those who had cash in the mattress, savings accounts in Canadian banks, and US government bonds slept well through the malaise. If 50% of their assets were exposed to assets that were melting down (peak to trough down 50%+), they were down less than 25% at the worst of the crisis. That is a significant draw down for anyone to take, but 50%+ would be, literally for most people, stomach churning! (How important is an honest personal inventory, especially regarding risk tolerance? You get the picture.)

Yet, look at where they are 3-4 years later. The major US stock market averages are up 100%, so those positions are, theoretically, whole. Commodities have rallied significantly as well. An investor's cash could have been put to work at depressed prices, but even if it wasn't the money was safe and the Canadian savings account paid interest throughout. Government bonds have been profitable investments too. Those well-balanced portfolios invested in multiple asset classes did relatively OK before the crisis, during the crisis, and post crisis.

Yes, even when it seems everything is crashing, usually there are asset classes that provide safety and, possibly, value. That is why it is good, along with taking an honest personal inventory, to allocate your assets in multiple asset classes. Who knows what is going up or down next year? No one, but you can use history to build a nice portfolio, one that allows you to sleep at night and hopefully puts you well on your way to meeting stated investment goals.

Here is a list of asset classes and subclasses:

Equity
    Domestic
    International
        Developed Country
        Emerging Markets
        Frontier Markets
            Small/Med/Large Market Capitalization (Market Cap = # of shares outstanding x share price)

Fixed Income
    Domestic
    International
        Preferred Shares
        Asset-backed Loans
        Senior Loans
        Subordinated Loans
        Bonds
            Corporate
            Government (Local, State, National)
                High-quality (AAA) to Default (D)
        Debentures
        Certificates of Deposit
        Money-market Funds

Commodities
    Soft (Wheat, Corn, Sugar...)
    Agriculture (Live/Feeder Cattle, Live Hogs, Pork Bellies...)
    Industrial (Copper, Platinum, Steel...)
    Precious Metals (Gold/Silver)
    Etc.

Collectibles
    Art
    Classic Cars
    Jewelry
    Baseball Cards
    Coin Collections
    Etc.

Derivatives
>   Futures/Options/Strips/et al

Cash
>   Mattress $, Safety Deposit Box, ~FDIC/private-insured accounts

Yikes! That does start to seem a little complex. Don't get overwhelmed; stay out of the weeds and focus on the top-level domains.

With regard to Equity and Fixed Income, it is important to understand two main things – where a security falls within the corporate capital structure & valuation.

Honestly, capital structure can get complex. I can't gloss over this fact. The details of securities contracts are voluminous, mundane, and usually written in Greek to the average guy. Don't despair, none of the fine details are really pertinent to you unless you are going into the world of high finance. That doesn't mean you shouldn't understand the basics. You just need to know where you stand in the capital structure so you understand your risk.

The easiest way to present this part is by listing in order who gets paid first if a company goes bankrupt (the essence of a company's capital structure).

Again, this is where the finance purists might nit-pick this presentation, but don't bother. We aren't preparing this for a Securities class. You just need to know how capital structure applies to you, and in general this is what it looks like –

Asset-backed Loan -   usually has a first lien on particular assets of the company.

Senior Loan -   usually backed by some collateral of the company that does not have a security interest placed on it.

Subordinated Loan -   usually a loan on an asset/ collateral that already has a (perfected) security interest placed on it.

Corporate Bonds -   where these rank in the hierarchy of outstanding bonds is disclosed in the offering memorandum.

Debentures -   usually low-man on the fixed-income totem pole when dealing with a bankruptcy.

Preferred Stock -   there can be separate classes of preferred stock which will be disclosed in the offering memorandum; always lower on the rung than debt holders and always above common stockholders.

Common Stock -	there can be separate classes of common stock as well, but separate classes usually deal with voting power more than anything; in capital structure common stock is at the bottom of the heap – everyone gets paid before this class of security holder.

As you can see owning common stock is not as glamorous as you may have once thought. The reason stock ownership is considered "risky" is not because there is some cabal at the stock exchange that works behind closed doors to steal unwitting investors' hard-earned money (traders do try to take advantage of retail investors but that is a different discussion entirely). Stock ownership is considered risky because its claims on the assets of the company are at the bottom of the capital structure.

In this book we won't go into valuing a company through all the different metrics. It's just too much information. Most young investors should start with mutual funds until they build up enough capital to properly allocate assets and diversify within those asset classes. Below a certain base amount, spending a lot of time and money diversifying one's portfolio reduces the effective return on invested capital. Doing so is a great learning experience, and hands-on training is very helpful in this arena, but it can be time and labor intensive, and it does exact transaction costs.

A general rule is if you are investing under $50,000 it is probably safe to say you should invest most of your money in mutual funds (take a little and learn the ropes by direct investing but don't risk a lot of your hard-earned money until you have become comfortable buying and selling individual securities). Once you eclipse the $50,000 threshold we will assume you have invested for a few years, learned some things, rode out some turbulence, and are ready to start doing more on your own. Realize that you never need to move out of mutual funds; they are great investment vehicles especially for long-term retirement accounts; but, there are a number of reasons to buy securities directly, not the least of these is the tax code – surprise, right? (A tax attorney or CPA can give you the skinny on mutual fund distributions and how they could effect your personal tax situation.)

As you build competence in security evaluation, being able to value an individual issuer (stock or bond) is important. Take Apple Inc. as an example. They carry no debt, have a lot of cash, and they generate huge sums of money every quarter. It is unlikely Apple will go bankrupt under this scenario. Compare APPL (trading symbol) to Fictional Company A, where A has very little cash on the balance sheet, 5x their revenue in debt, and they are losing money each quarter. While Apple's stock price could tumble in the short term because of geo-political events (a major country defaulting on its debt or a nuclear attack by a state-sponsored terrorist), the company is in a great position to handle such an external shock. It doesn't mean Apple's stock price would roar back to all-time highs soon after the shock, but the strength of Apple's financial position provides some long-term safeguards to your investment dollars.

Alternately, Company A is on a quick path to a default on their debt which would require a capital restructuring, which would likely end in a total wipe out of all common stockholders. Apple's stock price may trade at $500 and Company A at $5, but don't mistake price for value. Paying $500 for one share of Apple's stock would be infinitely wiser than paying $500 for 100 shares of Company A – there is just no comparison in value terms. That doesn't mean that Apple's stock couldn't trade down due to supply problems and Company A trades up based on pump-and-dump daytraders. Sure, you could make more money over the next month trading Company A stock versus Apple's stock under this scenario, but what are the comparative long-term prospects? Again, there is no comparison, none, not even a scintilla.

Valuation is absolutely most important when evaluating a security purchase. There are a lot of ways to measure value, and information is widely available on fundamental analysis of a company. What you should understand is that a company with a lot of cash, little debt and positive cash flow has some value today. The $64,000 question is what will the value of the company be tomorrow? And, as important, how much should you pay for that value? In general, Peter Lynch says 15x net income per share. Jim Cramer says 1.5x the company's growth rate. I might say 8x EBITDA. Candidly, banks are different than insurance companies, which are different than defense contractors, which are different than cable companies, which are different than retail chains, etc.

The big money (mutual funds, pension funds, hedge funds) measure companies in different industries with different metrics. Since big money moves the markets, you should evaluate companies using their metrics. Due to this nuance and the subjectivity of value in its own right, it is hard to give you a lot of good counsel without expanding the discussion significantly and going down into those proverbial weeds. So, you ask again, what is a good way to measure the value of a company? OK, here are a few metrics with which you can use as a foundation - A lot of cash relative to market cap; little or no debt; and positive, growing cash flow. You cannot go wrong with these simple baselines. What do you pay for such value? Mr. Lynch and Mr. Cramer provide two useful metrics for a broad swath of companies; it would be hard to argue with either's past performance.

If you are trading stocks, valuation may be a moot point. Short-term trading is less an economic value story and more a technical story, and that can be determined by many other factors than just value. However, over the long term, most demand will migrate toward the most valuable companies based upon the fundamentals of their total enterprise (products, intellectual property, management, financial statements, opportunities, etc.). Peter Lynch made a fortune for himself and his Fidelity Magellan investors by purchasing great companies at compelling valuations and holding them for long-term capital gains. Say what you want about Warren Buffett, but he became the richest man in the world by purchasing great companies at compelling valuations and holding them for long-term capital gains.

Not that you can't trade in milliseconds all day long and profit; a number of hedge funds do quite well at program trading. If you can replicate the returns of Renaissance Technologies I would suggest you do that for a few years. But for most of the general population, it would probably be better to hire guys like Mr. Lynch and Mr. Buffett to manage our money for us. And by hiring managers, who know value, we don't have to know every facet of every company to make a value judgment – we only have to understand the concept of valuation and assess whether our manager's are buying valuable companies at good "values". (Their performance will be an ongoing report card we can quickly scan for results.)

Proper asset allocation depends on your personal inventory (risk aversion, time frame, objectives, and cash flow). Since that is an individualized process I won't attempt customization (that's your job), but I will lay down some generalities with regard to our inventory score ranges and corresponding possible portfolios.

1-4 =	Totally Risk Averse (Only put the money under your mattress)
5-10 =	Very Conservative
11-20 =	Moderately Conservative
21-30 =	Conservative Growth
31-35 =	Aggressive
36-40 =	Very Aggressive

Totally Risk Averse –
100% - Cash, CDs, Insured Accounts, Short-term government bills

Very Conservative –
75% in the Totally Risk Averse portfolio
25% in Treasury Notes and A-rated short-medium term corporate fixed income

Moderately Conservative –
40% in the Totally Risk Averse portfolio
25% in Treasury Notes and A-rated short-medium term corporate fixed income
25% in high-quality, dividend-paying, blue-chip domestic equities
5% in medium to long-term investment grade corporate bonds
5% in commodities/hard assets

Conservative Growth –
15% in the Totally Risk Averse portfolio
20% in Treasury Notes and A-rated short-medium term corporate fixed income
25% in high-quality, dividend-paying, blue-chip domestic equities
20% in medium to long-term investment grade corporate bonds
10% in medium-large cap international equities
10% in commodities/hard assets

Aggressive –
10% in the Totally Risk Averse portfolio
20% in medium to long-term investment grade corporate bonds
20% in high-quality, dividend-paying, blue-chip domestic equities
20% in domestic small-medium cap stocks
20% in medium-large cap international equities
10% in commodities/hard assets

Very Aggressive –
10% in the Totally Risk Averse portfolio
10% in high-quality, dividend-paying, blue-chip domestic equities
20% in domestic small-medium cap stocks
30% in medium-large cap international equities
15% in commodities/hard assets
15% in a hedge fund/long-short mutual fund/derivatives-type fund

If you want a quick and simple investment plan, just determine your inventory scale and allocate your investment capital into a corresponding portfolio (above) of mutual funds. Of course I haven't recommended any funds or individual securities, but all you would have to do is call a Fidelity, Vanguard, American Century, Schwab, et al, mutual fund sales representative and discuss the portfolio(s) with them. They would be able to help you choose mutual funds that would meet most, if not all, of the criteria. Voila! You have an investment plan that is allocated properly based upon your personal inventory and by default (using broad-based mutual funds) you have diversification. You are set.

Now you just need to monitor the positions to make sure they perform up to your expectations. If you come to realize that your personal inventory has changed and therefore your score has changed, reallocate your assets suitably. If each position works well, and the portfolio tracks as you expect, you have a good plan. Be diligent as things always change; don't fret, just change accordingly.

Diversification

The idea behind diversification is so that one position/security will not hurt you too badly in case of a major problem. Just as asset allocation keeps you from being crushed by having all of your eggs in one asset class, within each asset class diversification further protects some of those eggs.

Systematic risk is defined as market risk. You can't really get away from market risk if you are in the markets, but you can manage the risk by allocating assets among different markets (stock market, bond market et al; among different asset classes), hopefully reducing correlation.

Unsystematic risk is defined as company risk. The market may be fine but a company's stock price may tank for many reasons; competitive threats, faulty execution, fraud, etc. Small biotechnology companies that have everything riding on an FDA approval can see their stock prices get beaten severely if a once promising trial ends up running into problems. Also, take a look at the different stock price trajectories of RIMM and APPL since Apple unveiled the iPhone in 2007. (RIMM was the hands-down leader in PDAs until Apple revolutionized the space.) And of course stories of WorldCom, Enron, Refco, etc. are infamous.

By purchasing multiple companies' securities, say in the large-cap, dividend-paying subclass of equities, you use diversification to reduce as much as possible your unsystematic risk. Of course there is no reason to buy 500 companies to reduce your risk, but you should buy ~10 to eliminate much of the company-specific risk. The problem with buying 500 companies is that you will probably end up with all of the dogs as well as the good ones, thereby hurting your overall performance. By focusing on the top-10 names (best of breed) in a particular subclass you are reducing unsystematic risk while not unnecessarily hindering your portfolio returns.

Does diversification limit your potential reward? It can. If your first choice was Apple, and then you purchased RIMM as well so that you didn't have all of your "apples" in one basket, then you definitely impaired your performance. However, if your first choice was RIMM, and then you purchased APPL to reduce company-specific risk, you improved your performance markedly over the last few years.

Don't misunderstand. Yes, when you reduce risk, by definition, you reduce your potential rewards. In practice, by putting APPL into your portfolio you actually improved performance quite dramatically while at the same time reduced unsystematic risk. (Great security selection is still a significant factor to overall returns.) This doesn't change the overriding principle of higher risk/higher reward, lower risk/lower reward. Optimization is always being sought, and there is an optimum portfolio at a static point in time.

Mutual funds are designed to provide automatic diversification, a big part of their value to individual investors.

Risk Management

Diversification is a way to manage unsystematic risk. Asset allocation reduces specific market risk. Yet, we want to manage risk more acutely; it is the one area where most people fall short.

First, let's define risk as exposure. If you are 100% invested in the stock market you have 100% of your capital at risk (exposed). Second, let's assume that we are only willing to risk a certain percentage of capital, say 10%. With this as our basis, it seems simple enough to keep 90% of capital in cash and invest 10% in the market. Sure, that can work, but by doing this you limit your upside quite a bit.

Let's flesh this out a little further. If the market doubles, you would earn 10% of your total portfolio (if only 10% of your portfolio was exposed to the market). If, however, you invest 100% of your portfolio in the stock market and the market increases 10%, you would earn the same 10% of your total portfolio. Granted, you took on 10x as much risk, but you only had to earn 1/10th as much. Hmmm...let's keep going and see what we come up with.

Over any arbitrary time frame (1 month, 1-year, 10-years) which do you think is more likely, the market doubling or the market increasing by 10%? It's a slightly loaded question as you can tell. Let me ask you another (unloaded) question - Is there a way to maximize potential upside while minimizing your downside risk?

Without knowing a lot about you I would never assume I could create a portfolio that would meet your needs. I also can't provide a strategy that fits with your emotional and psychological make up. Know Thyself is the appropriate thought here, meaning you know your personality and goals much better than anyone else. With that said, I am going to step out on a limb and tell you that you can be 100% exposed to the market, maximizing all potential upside, and still limit your downside to 10%. It's easy, if the market drops 10%, sell your total position. You have literally eliminated any further risk to your portfolio, and you were positioned to take full advantage of any upside.

There is a problem, though, with selling out completely - you would have no upside exposure going forward. You can't lose any more, but you can't make up any losses now either. This is quite a conundrum. And yes, there are no easy answers. I said investing didn't need to be complex; I never said there wouldn't be some difficult parts. Overall it is pretty easy, but risk management has some nuance to it. And, I will reiterate, it is vital to your success and most people miss the mark badly with regard to this concept.

So, what is the best way to manage price risk?

First, why is price important? It is important because price tells you the collective wisdom of the market. I am not a proponent of the Random Walk theory on markets; I believe there are many opportunities present in the market on any given day by its mispricing of individual securities. The word mispricing will raise many eyebrows. Yes, the market misprices many securities within the confines of a certain context. For that particular time period the market is 100% correct in its pricing, but that price (or its current direction) may not reflect accurately a stock price's future value (or direction). When you buy individual securities you should be purchasing the discounted value of the security's future price. Is that knowable? Of course not, it is 100% speculation, but that is what you are buying. As you are learning, assumptions are very much a part of this mad science.

What am I getting at? The market is always right in the moment and you never want to try to tell it how wrong it is because it will gladly take your money while you rant about its horrendous pricing error. The market will remain irrational much longer than you can remain solvent. Therefore, never try to "prove" anything to the market. Accept that the market is always 100% right, but Mr. Market does not have a crystal ball either. When he is irrational he is either providing you a great opportunity to buy or to sell, unless you are trying to prove him wrong in the moment, and then you are just donating your hard-earned money to his retirement fund. The point is that you must manage your risk according to your personal inventory and respond to changing circumstances as they arise.

Yes, I do realize it is a little odd to refer to the market almost as if it was a real person. The market is not a person, but then again it is – greed and fear drive him just like they do everybody because he is we, and our nature is imputed to him. In short order you will have your bouts with Mr. Market and may come to address him as I (and many others) do. At times he will seem to be your worst enemy, at other times he will seem to be your best friend. By understanding the market as a living entity you will better understand what drives the market to move; irrational gyrations will be less confusing.

So, again, what is the best way to manage price risk? Understand that managing price risk is essentially reducing exposure to a security, i.e., selling, usually. Therefore, managing price risk requires a selling discipline. When should a security be sold? It depends on your methodology.

Here are two examples:

1) Investor's Business Daily (IBD) promotes a system whereby a loss of 8% triggers a sell and a buy is only re-established once a security regains an uptrend.

2) Other systems will not sell at a pre-determined price or percentage loss and investors will only sell when a company is broken, meaning, when the company's fundamental story has changed unexpectedly (negatively).

These are completely different methodologies, and there are many others. You can modify one or the other to better fit your personality or your investment strategy. Just remember that closing out positions and going to cash is a viable option, and many times the best option (as you let the "dust" settle). There will always be opportunities in dynamic markets. However, if you lose all of your investment capital or scar yourself for life, you may not be in a position to take advantage of the numerous opportunities that will surface each year over your investing lifetime, and there will be a lot.

How do you manage your risk? You will need to determine that before you start investing. Don't dare invest a dime until you have a risk management system (asset allocation, diversification, selling discipline) in place. Then, continue to evaluate it and adjust accordingly. As you become more familiar with investing you will become more comfortable with the markets in general and portfolio management. This will result in a customized risk management system that best reflects your investor personality and goals.

Personally, with regard to a selling discipline, I like the idea of cutting losses (selling at pre-determined points), especially on individual securities, but I am more apt to be patient when dealing with mutual funds. They will still get whacked if the market craters – so goes the world of investing. Having proper asset allocation and diversification should reduce one's angst when things are a little testy, and it should allow the investor to patiently let the market work through its convulsions (which could take quarters or years).

Let me reiterate, when dealing with individual securities I would suggest cutting your losses unless you know the company and its business very well and have tremendous confidence in its management team, products and services. You can always purchase shares again if you want back in. That $5 commission ($10 round trip) will pale in comparison to the potential pain of a severe and possibly protracted downturn in the stock price. Pay your broker his pittance and reduce your exposure to risk. Even pros marry stocks, but they will tell you 100% of the time not to get so attached – here comes a cliché…it's not personal, it's just business. Really, it is only a transaction that you are engaging in to meet your investment objectives. Anything moving you away from meeting your goals should be scrutinized diligently, and cut loose quickly if necessary. Your goal is not to own pieces of paper but to increase your return on invested capital. One simple approach - Keep your winners, cut your losers, and never lose sight of the end game.

Summary – Foundational to your overall investment plan - you must take a personal investment inventory (Know Thyself). Once completed, and before you invest a dime, create an investment plan that will meet your investment objectives and that has a risk-management system (allocate properly, diversify appropriately, define a pre-determined selling discipline). Keep in mind that we are rational and emotional beings. Having a systematic risk-management process in place will reduce emotional investing errors. Do not invest any money until you are clear on your system of managing risk. And always remember that no one ever went broke by raising cash and questioning/reassessing a personal inventory and investment plan. Many have gone broke by not managing risk, by trying to prove Mr. Market wrong, and by "marrying" a security. Don't.

4.4: Start Now, Stay Disciplined, Seek Wise Counsel – "A wise man will hear and increase learning, and a man of understanding will attain wise counsel."

What are your financial priorities? These priorities will be the goals of your mini-portfolios we discussed in Section 4.2. Regardless of your list (down payment on a home, car purchase, trip around the world, build an orphanage, etc.), please start as soon as possible investing for your retirement. Time is such a valuable asset at this point in your life. Compounding interest (See Appendix C) is a powerful concept, and one you should leverage while time is still an asset and not a liability. Even if it is only $50 per month, start ASAP. It is that important.

One, you want to get in the habit of paying yourself first by investing in your future. Two, the habit will turn into a discipline which you likely will not violate, at least not without much thought and reflection. Put "retirement account" at the top of your personal budget, the first "expenditure" of your income, before mortgage/rent, utilities, food, etc. Make it a top priority if at all possible, with the exception of charitable giving. (Giving your income to worthy causes [religious organizations, relief organizations, community food banks/clothes closets, etc.] will always make you grateful for what you have and keep you grounded, and of course alleviating human suffering is always a tremendous investment regardless of your age, gender, nationality, ethnicity, politics, socio-economics, geography, etc.)

Fifty dollars per month invested over 40 years earning 8% on average would build up to $174,550. Total investment would equal only $24,000; $150,000 would be earnings compounded! Commit to $50 per month as soon as possible. ($100 over 40 years at 10% would equal $632,407; total investment would be $48,000; $584,000 would be earnings compounded – half a million dollars!)

How does one get started? If you have a 401k at work, put as much as you can into the plan. If possible, and if your company matches your contributions, put in at least as much as the match. As an example, if the company match is up to 3%, make sure and put in at least 3% of your annual salary. If your salary is $30,000, 3% is $900. If you invest $900 your company will match the $900, effectively doubling your investment immediately. This is a huge advantage. Put as much back as you can and take full advantage of your company's matching program. Your HR personnel will give you all the information you need to get started.

If you do not have a company plan, invest in an IRA or Roth IRA. Put as much back as you can. An IRA is self-directed, so instead of investing through a company plan, you would be able to open an account with most any investment firm (Vanguard, American Century, Schwab, et al) online and start investing immediately. You can invest in mutual funds, ETF's, stocks, bonds, etc. IRA's are Individual Retirement Accounts. An IRA is not an investment; it is a vehicle under which you can make investments. It is a tax designation (like a 401k or 403b, areas of the code where you can find parameters of these investment vehicles) that treats these investment dollars separately than say an Individual brokerage account. Again, IRAs are not investments, they are designated accounts/vehicles in which personal retirement investments can be made.

Get online and go to American Century's or Schwab's web site. They have information on IRAs; read through it. Then, check out other mutual fund company web sites (Vanguard et al) and their IRA information as well. You can download the IRA application and send it in. It's a very simple process. If you would feel more comfortable speaking to a representative, give one of the companies a call. They usually have very nice and helpful reps always available.

Once you have your retirement account set up and you are depositing funds monthly, you should prioritize your other investment goals and start setting up accounts/portfolios for each.

Emergency savings account – how much? That is up to you. Try to get a few thousand dollars built up as soon as possible. The last thing you want to be forced into paying is credit card interest rates for emergencies – a quick way to get behind the eight ball. Anytime you tap it for emergencies make sure and re-fund it as quickly as possible. These funds should be safe and liquid; cash in your mattress, savings account.

Reserve savings account – Get at least 3 months of expenses put back as soon as possible. Many financial pros encourage building up a 6-month reserve account, but it wouldn't hurt to get it to 12 months. You never know when you may be furloughed or let go; the economy can change very quickly. You don't want to lose your residence or be unable to pay for basic necessities if there is an interruption in your income stream. These funds should be safe and liquid.

Car account – As we discussed before, instead of paying interest on a depreciating asset like a car, make a "monthly car payment" into your car investment fund/mini-portfolio and "earn interest" while building it up until you can pay cash for your vehicle. This account is longer term so your investment choices can expand (depending on your complete personal inventory). This is a 3-10 year fund - it is reasonable to take more risk as you seek higher returns than savings accounts.

You might, most likely do, have many other investment objectives. Prioritize them and fund them accordingly. There are three primary keys to success: 1) Just do it (prioritize and get each set up independently); 2) Be disciplined (fund each habitually until it becomes engrained in your persona); and 3) Know Thyself (invest according to risk tolerance, time frame, objective and cash/cash flow). It is not complex or difficult to do; it is simple and only a matter of personal fortitude. The choice to be financially successful is yours alone.

Because investing is not difficult and there are volumes of information easily accessible via the internet, anyone of sound mind can take on the task independently. However, there is nothing wrong with hiring a professional advisor to assist you. One-on-one consulting is expensive. There is no way to get around the economics of the business. Yet, if you find an advisor who provides more value than the price of services rendered, don't feel compelled to go it alone if you are uncomfortable. Value is subjective, so I can't give you a formula, but you are smart enough to assess the value of one's services.

Thanks to our advanced communications infrastructure you have the opportunity to network with other individual investors, professionals, and institutions right from your home. Of course you can use old technology (phone) to call a live representative at a number of firms as I have described previously to discuss investing, and these call centers are provided for free for prospective investors. (Current investors in the funds pay for these reps indirectly through fees; you will too if you invest in the funds.) The cost, if any, is minor compared to in-person financial advice. And of course forums, blogs, chats, etc. are mostly available for free online. Additionally, <u>Forbes</u>, <u>Kiplinger's</u>, <u>Investor's Business Daily</u> et al have very good investment information available, usually for a subscription fee. Lastly, there are untold niche web sites that provide substantial financial information at different rates (free to low-cost to premium subscriptions), such as <u>4t Nox U</u>, <u>Motley Fool</u>, <u>The Street.com</u>, <u>Minyanville</u>, etc.

The point is that help is available from a variety of sources. If you are not yet comfortable going it alone, just search, ask, and chat. There is no reason you should ever use the excuse that you "would have but didn't know how to get started." It has been said that there are no dumb questions. Well, let's be honest, that isn't exactly true. Sure there are, but they usually do not come from people genuinely interested in learning something; they usually come from a guy just shooting off his mouth (ego, posture, general inanity…). Ask as many questions as you can to as many different sources as possible and discern helpful information and nice people from useless information and rude people. Don't let ignorance be an excuse to fail, only an excuse to learn.

Summary – Prioritize, Be Disciplined, Know Thyself; always be in learning mode; and just do it.

DISCUSSION 5: HOME OWNERSHIP

It's actually a good idea

5.1: The American Dream – Property, pride, community.

What is "The American Dream?" I suppose there are numerous definitions; it probably depends on who you are speaking with and what their experience/influence has been. Some probably see it through a purely material lens. Others likely view it as opportunity for a better life. I would bet there are those who believe it is a myth, or a concept of days gone by, or, maybe at best, an idea for those who already have "made it" but not accessible to anyone else.

Just so we are on the same page I will provide a working description for our purposes. The American Dream is what sets us apart from citizens of any other country and why so many people still try to immigrate. It has been engrained in our psyche from the very outset. We are graced with a history of freedom – we are free to pursue our dreams with very few institutional obstacles. Each succeeding generation has seen those few obvious obstacles removed, some slowly, but removed nonetheless. This idea of freedom cannot be expressed any better than it was 236 years ago – "We hold these truths to be self-evident, that all men are created equal, that they are endowed by their Creator with certain unalienable Rights, that among these are Life, Liberty and the Pursuit of Happiness..." Our national heritage promotes the unique individuality of mankind, it encourages the most positive aspects of human nature. This Great Experiment worked because it aligned certain governing principles with man's unalienable rights. Because of this alignment millions of people poured onto our shores begging for the opportunity to be free and to pursue their dreams as they defined them. It is the greatest gift – freedom - we could have been bequeathed.

Included in the American DNA is the sacrosanct idea of private property; tyrants, monarchs, governments, etc. do not have a divine right to our property. Government was instituted primarily to defend our rights to life, liberty and property from internal and external forces – other countries, criminals, and bullies; and, today unfortunately, in an odd twist, it fights to protect us against much of its own <u>bureaucracy</u>. The Declaration goes on to say, "That to secure these rights, Governments are instituted among Men, deriving their just powers from the consent of the governed. That whenever any Form of Government becomes destructive of these ends, it is the Right of the People to alter or to abolish it, and to institute new Government, laying its foundation on such principles and organizing its powers in such form, as to them shall seem most likely to effect their Safety and Happiness." Our whole political, economic, and social system was developed around the idea of protecting these rights. Under such a system the United States of America became the most prosperous and powerful country the world has ever seen, and we did it in less than 200 years. That is a phenomenal accomplishment, absolutely unparalleled in the annals of history. Yes, imperfect, yes, with many scars, but through all of the imperfections we have become a more perfect union.

The American Dream is the belief that we can define success as we choose, independent of others, that we have the right to pursue our individual dreams as long as we do not infringe on another's rights, and that we are assured, institutionally, by our social contract, that the fruits of our labor are ours to be kept, used, and distributed as we see fit. Yes, the American Dream is opportunity, opportunity to succeed and fail, and to try again. But it is so much more than that. Americans have a unique heritage, one that promotes man's individual nature, spirit, and desire, and one that created a political, economic and social structure which supported such. As citizens we all have equal rights of life and liberty and to opportunity under the law. U.S. citizenship is, and should be considered, special.

The American Dream is not by its origin one of materialism; rather, it is an ideal that has been proven to unleash human ingenuity and industry which results in prosperity. Wouldn't it be shallow and sad to define the American Dream as materialism, or as a long-lost ideal, or that which only applies to a chosen few? I think so. Thankfully, that is not the case, at least not today. Yet, there is no guarantee that the success of the Great Experiment will last forever. As unique as it has been to history it would not be surprising to see it as only a blip on an historical chart some centuries in the future. The blip may have a footnote that states – "Freedom was tried for a few hundred years in the former U.S.A., but it didn't work; it was a failed experiment which imploded due to apathy on the one end and insatiable greed on the other. Man cannot handle his own independence and must be managed by a collective (a ruling class, a monarch)."

Make sure you understand your heritage as an American, embrace it, and build upon it. Apathy and/or insatiable greed very well could lead to collective management which is antithetical to our national identity. It would be a shame to go down in history with the above footnote. That is not what we were, who we are, or what we are capable of.....we are the flag bearer's of freedom and should carry that mantle proudly.

OK, granted, so what does that have to do with home ownership? I am sure you have already connected the dots, but I will present an answer anyway, if nothing more than a reiteration of what you already know. Home ownership is a huge part of the American Dream because you own it; it is your castle; you are the chief executive, the legislator, the judge and the jury in your own home. You are not a serf beholden to the lord of the land (landlord). You should have a healthy pride in owning your own home. You should understand the deep philosophical nature of private property and its importance in a free society. There is nothing wrong with renting a place, and renting serves a good purpose for many situations, but there is a huge psychological difference between being a tenant and a land owner.

Along with psychology and pride, owning a home in a neighborhood, town or county gives you a sense of community. You are a member who has a huge stake in the quality of its governance, schools, roads, etc. You own the dirt and expect things to be handled a certain way, a way in which property values are maintained (yours and your neighbors). The permanence of ownership instills a certain longevity and/or commitment which many times translate to a stronger sense of community. Of course renters are valuable members of the community and always will be; there is just a fundamental difference between renting and owning.

Think of it this way - do you treat the car you own the same way you treat a rental car? This is not to be considered a direct parallel, but the gist of the idea is valid. When you have to work and scrap for every dime to purchase your new car there is a certain pride of ownership. How do you feel after that first door ding? It's just a car and gets you from point A to point B. A little ding here or there isn't that significant, right? Wrong, of course it is. A dent on the rental car doesn't faze you at all, but a scratch, ding, dent on your new car rubs you the wrong way.

That's the power of private property ownership – you care, a lot; and that type of responsible self-interest permeates in varying degrees and forms throughout all society. Unquestionably, it has a positive multiplier effect. Owning a home is a very big part of the American Dream; it is a healthy and natural desire. Candidly, it will be the most valuable single asset of most people in our country. And that is a very big deal.

Summary – Home ownership instills a sense of pride and community. It has a positive psychological effect that permeates throughout our society. The American Dream is alive and well, and home ownership is a very big part of it.

5.2: Buy Right – Attack the purchase like 'Extreme Couponers'.

"That guy just has the Midas touch." "She is as lucky as they come." I have heard other people say, not with a covetous heart in the least, similar things about people who seem to make good business/financial decisions. Many times we don't quite understand how that guy always ends up on top. The reality is that he doesn't always make profitable investments. We usually only see or hear about the good ones. Every successful person I know has had difficult challenges, and they have their fair share of failures. The real difference between the "lucky ones" and those not as fortunate usually comes down to two things: attempts and work ethic.

Successful people shoot the ball a lot; they aren't afraid of failure. I remember being in awe of Michael Jordan when he would put up 30 or 40 points consistently. I would ask myself, "How can a guy do that every night against the best players in the game?" Granted, he was one of the best ever to lace up some Nike's. But, in my quantitative quest for more detail, I started looking through the box scores more frequently. I noticed that he would shoot 12 for 30 from the field (with a few three pointers and a dozen or so free throws) and end up with 40 points. I never really thought a guy shooting 40% was a very special player. I mean a few of those shots were slam dunks, so how hard could it be to shoot 40%. A lot of guys shoot 40% or better from the field, but they are not Michael Jordan. What made him what he was? Simplistically, he shot the ball more than anyone else; it was basic arithmetic.

Continuing with MJ – he also had a tremendous work ethic. And I don't just mean working hard at practice. I will assume anyone who makes it in the NBA has spent substantial time on a basketball court. I suspect they have shot countless free throws in the rain at night, alone. But did anyone work harder at getting the ball during the game than Jordan? Again, I suppose many of his teammates worked hard at getting open too. He got the ball because he was willing to make the shot when other guys would rather pass. He got the ball because he demanded he get the ball, because he was willing to risk failure to make the shot. His teammates gladly passed him the ball because more often than not he would make the shot! And they knew he would pass them the ball if necessary to win the game – he wanted to win more than he needed to be the star, and in so doing he became a living legend. My point is that Jordan worked hard, and in so doing he gained confidence in his competence, which translated to his teammates having confidence in him. He would take the shot anytime opportunity was presented, and many times he would create his own opportunities. Also, he always kept his focus on the ultimate goal – winning – and would share the rock with any of his mates to achieve that goal.

Very few people are Air Jordan, but remember, Michael wasn't Air when he was a freshman in high school. He worked his tail off so he could "get lucky". You don't have to become the best in the world at anything, but if you commit to working hard and are willing to "take the shot" (and keep shooting), you have a much better chance at success in whatever you decide to do. Granted, not everyone's fate is equal, and sometimes outcomes do not correspond with inputs – that is a hard fact of life. However, I can assure you that your chances of success go up significantly if you work hard and keep trying.

How does this have anything to do with home ownership? Recall that this section is about buying right. Many people undertake investing and researching a home purchase with less effort than they exert in playing video games or buying clothes. With investing, they would rather be lazy and lucky (see as gambling) than spend time managing their portfolio. When purchasing a home people leave it to their real estate broker to do the heavy lifting. While many brokers are professional in their approach and run their businesses with integrity, their main goal is to close transactions – the more at higher prices the better. It's not wrong; it's just their business. They have to pay their bills as well. I would suggest leaning on a broker to sell your home makes more sense than on the buy side. (Don't get me wrong; if you can find one who will dig long and deep to present you with the best deal in the area, leverage them big time, just don't expect that as typical. Most approach the business as service providers – they are called brokers - rather than investors due to the economics of the profession. It's just the nature of the business. If you find one with an investor mentality, great, but that would be atypical.)

When making that single-largest purchase in your life, I believe it would behoove you to be much more involved in the process. With the internet you can easily find out a lot of information fairly quickly. Many counties have property information online today. It's easy to find out particulars about properties, neighborhoods, areas, etc. – home sales, prices, owners, activity... There are also a number of real estate research sites available. Don't expect to luck into a great deal, and don't expect your real estate broker to care as much about your financial well-being as you do. Roll up your sleeves and get to work. If you are looking to buy a home you had better make sure you know the ins-and-outs of the area. How many houses are for sale? What is the average sale price per foot? How long are they sitting on the market? How does price compare to rents, cost-to-build and other area housing markets? Because real estate is local, there are not any easy ways to overlay a specific value model; e.g., $70 per foot is a good value; $150 per foot is expensive. In Oklahoma City $150/ft gets you a little more than it does in New York City. It takes work to know your market and to search for deals that make sense in your locale. There is no way in getting around it, that is, if you want to be a good personal financial manager.

It's not rocket science; it just takes a little elbow grease. If you want to find a good deal, you need to do the work necessary to make it happen. I have watched a cable show of extreme couponers a couple of times. Those people are amazing; sometimes they pay $1.50 for $150 worth of groceries. It is unbelievable, but I could do the same thing. I just don't choose to invest the time necessary to have that type of shopping success. I tell my wife she should do that. Of course, she tells me she would if I would help her, which ends any chance of it ever happening. It takes hard work and a sincere commitment. How much more dedicated should you be when making a six-figure home purchase?

Too many times people are not willing to do the work because there is a chance an offer will not be accepted. This gets back to MJ's shot attempts. Work hard, do your homework, decide what price makes sense for you (a smart financial decision), and then make an offer. If it doesn't work out, go through the same process time and again. If you can save tens of thousands of dollars of principal and two or three times that in interest payments, is it worth spending the time? If not, don't worry about it. If so, make a commitment to work hard and be disciplined, and keep taking shots. Please, don't let the extreme couponers outwork you when it comes to making one of the largest single purchases you will ever transact!

Summary – Finding a good deal (buying right) isn't about luck; it's about hard work and persistence. You should spend exponentially more time on research when purchasing a home than on playing video games or buying clothes. More than likely it will be the single biggest purchase you'll ever make – Treat it seriously.

5.3: Own a home – Make some memories.

You never want to get caught up in a bubble and lose 50% on your home purchase. That is a nightmare. The financial and psychological repercussions of such an experience would be lasting and extremely challenging. Of course hindsight is 20/20, but as young adults you can learn from others' mistakes.

When engineers leave their profession to start flipping homes, you are probably living in a bubble. I actually had an old acquaintance do just that. He went to school at Arizona State University. He is a sharp guy who received an engineering degree and worked in the Phoenix area. He told me he quit engineering to go into real estate because he could make three times as much flipping houses. As a matter of fact, he said he sold a house for a nice profit the day after he closed his purchase, and he did this more than once. In the internet bubble, many people thought there was a whole new business paradigm and the "old way" was being replaced. It was a new paradigm, but eyeballs needed to translate into "old way" profits or businesses would fail, which many, many, many did. Unsurprisingly, normal housing markets are not characterized by 100%

annual turnover rates. Profits still matter in the new internet paradigm just as basic supply and demand still apply in housing.

Speculative bubbles create tremendous opportunities for traders and those owners (regardless of the product – homes, cattle, oil, gold, tulips, etc.) who sell into it. Obviously Phoenix-area real estate was in a bubble. Potential new buyers could sit on the sidelines and rent until the game was up or play the game, but buying at the top of a bubble is almost always devastating. The problem with the game is that no one knows when the top will climax, and sitting on the sidelines watching engineers triple their incomes drives people to make very emotional decisions. (Greed and fear have always been and always will be powerful drivers.) Take away – Be careful when profits are made easily in a new paradigm and old business metrics are eschewed – no better sign of a probable bubble. If you find yourself in a possible bubble, tread carefully and be very diligent when considering a large, long-term investment. No two bubbles are the same, but they all have similar characteristics, and the temptations are strong. And who doesn't like to make easy money? If it is too good to be true and reason seems to be set aside for a "new paradigm" and/or "guaranteed" starts to get used frequently, go ahead and assume something is fishy, become cautious, and always be vigilant.

With that said, let's approach home ownership as something more than flipping houses in a speculative bubble. (Assume, though, that bubbles will always come and go in stocks, bonds, real estate, commodities, baseball cards, tulips, &Etc.---human nature doesn't change.)

Owning a home is part of the American Dream. I encourage you to set it as one of your goals. Become a concerned landowner in your community. Get involved in little league baseball, your church, your local political precinct, etc. Life is meant to be lived and shared amongst people, not in dark rooms with avatars or digital "friends". Not that new social communities do not have a place in the 21st century, obviously they do. Leverage available technologies as much as you are comfortable to broaden your connectivity base. Develop relationships with people you would have never met otherwise – share with, learn from, teach and influence them. The scale of the internet is phenomenal. But, don't forget that live human interaction is still the cornerstone of building a strong relationship. Owning a home and getting involved in your local community will still be the primary way for you to influence your environment in a positive way. Will that paradigm change in the 22nd century? A lot will change between now and then, but I doubt my basic premise gets altered. Of course I really don't know and frankly don't care; my great (great)-grandchildren will have to navigate that dynamic. Even if it did change so dramatically that live interaction was a bother, what does it matter to my wife, kids, friends, and associates? They need to engage in the world that is, as do you, and our world thrives on live, personal, intimate relationships. Being a landowner gives you a perfect opportunity (and reason) to get involved.

There are two ways to own a home – buy one or build one (assuming you are not going to have one given to you). We discussed buying previously. Ask a lot of questions and do a lot of research pretty much sums up the antecedents to a home purchase. Building a home is a bit different - Hard work is not just imagery or a mental construct; in this context hard work should be defined literally. Building a home is frustrating, challenging, painstaking, exciting and rewarding. And, unfortunately, sometimes it can turn costly.

My wife and I built our first home. We are still in it today. My brother-in-law and sister-in-law built their first homes too. I have quite a few friends who have done so as well. It is very doable. If we can do it, anybody can do it. Though, your geographic location may have institutional barriers to entry for do-it-yourselfers. In that case, you can sub-contract it all out as the general contractor, or you can hire a general contractor to manage the project. Just as with investing (stock broker) and buying a home (real estate broker), no general contractor will have your financial interests as their primary concern. That's not a bad thing; it just is. Don't ever expect someone else to care as much about your financial situation/future as you do.

What does it take to build a home? It takes a lot of planning, organization, time and hard work. The very first thing we did was buy a book from Home Depot. Honestly. It was specifically targeted to people who wanted to build their own home. And while some of the projected expenses were off one way or another, dramatically at times, the overall cost was close enough to be workable with regard to financial planning. If you have any inclination to do such a thing, I recommend buying a book and working with your local building supply store. Those guys were very helpful in my opinion. Our local Home Depot used to give free Saturday sessions (probably still do) on all kinds of things; laying tile, painting, decking, etc.

The focus of this book would broaden way too much if I was to go into detail about homebuilding (there are seemingly endless details). I could give you bulging files of our two-decades old stuff as we still have it stored somewhere, but I think it best for you to seek wiser counsel with regard to the whole process in your area, i.e., buy your own book with up-to-date information or talk to others in your community who have navigated this trip. However, I do want to discuss two more things regarding this topic.

First, I would suggest seriously looking into building your own home if you have the wherewithal to take on such a demanding project. If you do it right and well, it may be possible to save a significant amount of money (5%-20%), and you will create a number of priceless (hilarious/infamous) memories in the process. Even through all the challenges, we had a blast, but today is a totally different environment - **You may be able to pick up a new/fairly new home that meets your needs for much less than it costs to build.** And realize that it is highly likely that you will not do it nearly as well as a seasoned professional, and that you will spend significantly more time over the next year than you plan – if that is a problem, just buy.

Second, all of your relationships have the potential to be strained. There were disagreements and misunderstandings with my wife, father-in-law, roofer, door supplier, window supplier, and electrician, and surely more if I had better recall. It was really cool once we were finished, but there are many things we would change if we could. There is an old saying that it takes three times to actually build a house exactly the way you want it. I would grant some exceptions to that statement, but on average that is probably an accurate figure. Unknowingly to a first-time amateur, there are many subtleties inherent in such a diversified project. Centering light fixtures in the bathrooms can be an easy item to overlook. Framing and wiring are instrumental in getting the fixtures centered. (Yes, the plans lay out everything on paper, but it is amazing that sometimes even the best laid plans don't get executed exactly right.) Who would have thought someone could mess that up? (Never assume anything; and, trust but verify.)

As a quick eye-opener here is a short list of some pre-planning:

General Contractor Resource (book)
Land Purchase
Proper zoning of the land (city planner)
House plans (quadruplicate x2 – everyone needs to see the plans)
Construction financing in place (bank)
Plan approval by city (submit plans in triplicate)
Building permit (permit number posted publicly)

Now you are ready to start. Here are a few tips:

Plan for 3 draws from the bank and make sure and add in your interest charges (Good to have each phase projected financially so the banker can easily check and assess your progress to approve each subsequent draw)

Being a general contractor sounds pretty easy – just hire subs, right? Not quite. You have to understand the sequence of tasks and schedule accordingly. It also helps to have a list of subs available, which you probably don't. And, as the GC, you need to know when something is not being done according to plan. It is expensive to rework a framing miscue once wiring, insulation and sheet rock have been completed! As a GC, you need to be well-organized, aggressive at following up, and have an acute attention to detail. You can't get around it. If these are skills you don't possess, it would be better to hire a reputable GC.

Start lining up sub-contractors – Warning: Some of these guys are great, some not so much... Additionally, many of them have help that may not always show up every day on time – just the nature of the field. (The 'guide book' was essential – _essential_ – when it came to a schedule; we were never on time because of sporadic subs and our own slow work, but we did know what task needed to be done and when so we could plan accordingly as best as possible.)

Being your own sub-contractor can be financially helpful, but your time on task may be extended versus a professional crew and your (lack of) skill may cost you more in the long run. Do what you can do (say painting and rolling insulation); go ahead and hire what you can't do (say sheet rock, plumbing). Of course this is completely predicated on your skill set and experience. If you have no experience and no trade skill and are incapable of learning to lay insulation, you will save yourself heartache and money by hiring professionals. A six month build can easily turn into 12 months, which means additional interest expense – usually not too detrimental to your budget, but you should recognize the cost.

As a young couple we saved a small fortune, had a memorable time, and we were very proud of our accomplishment, but it is not a project for everyone. Without help from a lot of family and friends, we never would have been able to do it, and it still took us twice as long as a professional builder. We didn't have any kids, so we could devote most of our free time to the house. Also, we had been married about 8 years and got along well. The strains of the project could easily flow over and cause deep marital fissures, especially if that metaphorical foundation already had cracks in it. There is another old saying about building your own home: "If your marriage can withstand building a house together it can withstand anything." I wouldn't agree totally with that assessment, but there is definitely a strain of truth to it.

All-in-all, we thought it was well worth the effort. Whether you build or buy, I encourage you to take part in that slice of the American Dream. Home ownership is pretty special. Since completion we have brought two little babies home from the hospital. We have had 8 Christmas mornings watching kids open presents. We have made snow angels and snowmen in the front yard. We have set up 3D silhouette archery targets in the back yard and shot a thousand arrows. Birthday parties, anniversaries, game days, towel fights, garden "harvests", etc. We have untold numbers of pictures and video clips of particular events with our home as the main backdrop. These things (and many, many more) have been done at a place our kids can call their own.

Of course families can do the same things in rentals for sure, and they should create memories wherever they're at. Candidly, every time I think of how fortunate we are I am humbled. We have been blessed. We rented for the first eight years of our marriage as we saved for a down payment - Just two middle class kids starting out on an exciting life journey, creating memories whenever we could wherever we were at, working hard to make our way. Regardless of whether homeownership is on the immediate horizon, you should start creating family history wherever you are at in a loving place that you call home because building relationships and creating lasting memories are the real goals. Relationships are lasting, more so than temporary structures that can vanish in a tornadic instant. But, based upon my experience as a kid and now as a parent, if at all possible (only at the right time for you), I encourage you to own your own home. It's not "The American Dream", but being the King/Queen in your own castle is definitely one important part of it.

Summary – Try to recognize potential bubbles and act accordingly with regard to your investments. If anything seems too easy or too good to be true, it probably needs further investigation and likely needs to be avoided, unless you are into gambling with your hard-earned money. Build your own home if you have the ability to do so, but only if it makes sense personally and financially. Become a part of the community in which you live and have a positive impact. Regardless of whether you own or rent, build relationships and create memories; focus first on those things that are most important and lasting. And, when possible, consider owning a home – it is an important part of the American Dream.

For more information on getting a mortgage or a lease, see Appendix D & E, respectively.

DISCUSSION 6: INSURANCE

A necessary evil.....and your bedrock to personal risk management

6.1: Insurance Poor – It shouldn't cost an arm and a leg but it does.

If you sell insurance I am sure you have frequently heard the line, "I'm insurance poor." While that phrase may sound like opportunity to a creative insurance agent/broker - a prospect who has a pain point and needs some advice - it is usually a pre-programmed defensive line from the potential customer. In reality, many people are insurance poor, and if presented with a better value they would listen intently; I know I would.

Insurance is one of those expenses that weigh on most rational minds. You purchase something every year hoping you don't actually have to use it. Isn't that a weird phenomenon? I think it is. You are rooting for the company to keep all of your premium money, and they are rooting for the same thing - the table is turned topsy-turvy in this particular vender-customer relationship. As the customer you would expect to receive value, or there is no reason to be in the relationship. But, to receive that value something (usually bad) has to happen. What's the alternative? Don't purchase insurance and then when something "bad" does happen you carry the full weight of the expense. That doesn't seem prudent.

The whole dynamic is slightly odd, even counter-intuitive on its surface. Even so, insurance is essential, which is the very reason it has been such a profitable industry for so long, especially when underwriting models are accurate. Berkshire Hathaway owns a lot of companies, and I am sure Mr. Buffett loves eating See's candy and drinking Coke (a Berkshire company and an investment, respectively), but I suspect the Oracle of Omaha's insurance holdings are the ones he would rather not be without. He loves cash, and they definitely generate a lot of it!

In the following paragraphs I will expand on this discussion just a bit more, but in the end the gist of it is pretty straightforward. As much as I hate to say it, and every time I say it I will do so begrudgingly, go ahead and bite the bullet each year and buy as much insurance as you need and can afford to properly manage your risks. Insurance poor or not, you must manage all risks that could negatively impact your net worth.

Let me give you an example of how one can be insurance poor:

A young graduate is an accountant at a small midwestern business. The small company only has 20 employees and can't afford to provide health, disability, or life insurance, though it does subsidize its employees' independent purchases by giving each one an additional $200 per month.

The young accountant makes $42,000 per year (salary plus insurance subsidy). He has a wife and two young children

124

at home. Due to the <u>tax code morass</u> (we actually have a <u>National Taxpayer Advocate</u> office within the IRS) we won't try to determine his after-tax income; for simplicity's sake, we will <u>assume</u> he is part of the 47% of Americans who pay <u>no federal income tax</u>, and we'll assume he doesn't pay any state income tax either. His share of the FICA tax is about $3,000, so we know he gets home with approximately $3,300 each month. Not bad, but what does it look like after he pays his insurance premiums?

For a family of four with a $1,500 annual deductible, our accountant pays $1,000 per month in health insurance. His homeowner's insurance policy runs him $1,000 per year. He and his wife's life insurance policies cost about $25 per month and his automobile policies cost $2,500 annually. His grand total is $15,800 per year! And this doesn't include a short-term and long-term disability policy which would provide some sort of salary protection if he was to miss work due to an unfortunate accident. (He can't afford it; there is no money left at the end of the month for his medical deductible, if needed, or for the kids' college savings fund, much less a disability policy.) Forty percent of his bring-home income goes to insurance premiums! 40%! That's a huge hit to anyone's standard of living.

Obviously the big kahuna is the health insurance premium. Without getting into a deep policy discussion, it is obvious our health insurance market is unsustainable. Insurance will never be a great financial investment by a majority of the population (the business model wouldn't work if that was the case), but adequate health insurance coverage for a middle-class family of four shouldn't cost 30% of income. That's patently absurd. Mandates, third-party payer systems, a lack of competition and tort misuse all play a significant part in the inflated costs of health insurance. Major reform is necessary and will bring us, as a society, to a fork in the road; one of two paths will be followed – one path leads to much less government regulation and more competition, the other to a nationalized healthcare system. The current "middle way" is not politically, economically, or socially feasible.

I am generally opposed to all-things-nationalized. I just don't think that is a type of system which promotes individual liberty, and I am first and foremost and forever in support of independence, whether that be a complete split from an English monarch or a massive devolution of US national bureaucracy. But, I understand how our young accountant could be torn between freedom and security, if just on a personal financial level. And if he never asks a deeper question than "how much will that benefit me financially today," he will usually lean toward subsidized dependence. I believe it's a shallow and wrong position, but it is certainly understandable from one perspective. (Of course I believe answers to a multi-level tier of questions will naturally argue against nationalization – Why are healthcare costs so expensive? Why is health insurance so expensive? Who should pay for healthcare? [Search – publicly or privately - these three direct questions and you will retrieve a slew of opinions.] How are those payments extracted? Where could that money have been otherwise directed? Who makes those decisions? What did I give up [independence] for this benefit [security]? Where does this path logically lead? Does it promote a free peoples or an institutionalized dependency?)

Because reform is still off in the distance, how could our accountant cope with his current financial dilemma? He could continue to live off of $1,800 per month (after-insurance-premium income) making due with what he has; he could get a second job to provide some much needed income; he could start a side business selling his accounting services on a contract basis – All difficult but decent options depending on family goals. He could choose not to purchase insurance and allow the Medicaid system to "kick in" if a major medical emergency impacted his family or the bankruptcy system to resolve any unpaid medical expenses – This does happen, but most would say this is not the best option if it can be avoided. He could increase his deductible on the health insurance policy (to say, $10,000) and reduce his monthly premium. This type of major medical policy would cover costs after he covers the first $10,000 of expenses each year. The premiums might run him $300-$400 per month. An additional $700 per month (old premium minus new premium) of "income" would be helpful, and makes a lot of sense, but he needs to have an insurance fund established with $10,000 to cover his part each year. It is possible that, barring a major medical expense, premium savings less annual medical costs could get this "deductible fund" fully funded in a couple years. Clearly, there are no easy answers, but fortunately there are options.

Our accountant has a number of choices, some better than others. Maybe he combines a few to get by. Everyone's situation is different, but when someone says he is insurance poor, make no mistake, the middle class family that tries to manage its risk prudently is being put under great financial pressure. Poor may not be the most accurate term, but relatively speaking it works as a description of the effect of insurance premiums on middle-class families.

Now, truth be told, if anyone painted you a picture of an easy life, they didn't tell you the whole story. Living is great, and living in America is pretty cool, but no one should expect fields of milk and honey without sacrifice. Life will provide you many challenges and blessings, many obstacles and rewards, regardless of where you live. That's just life. And while we moan about costs of insurance, we at least have the opportunity to purchase it; and while we gripe about healthcare costs, even the poorest Americans receive better care than the average global citizen. We shouldn't be satisfied, because there is no doubt the system could be better, but we should express a certain level of content and gratitude. On average we don't have it all that bad.

Summary – Insurance is an odd deal, one where the customer cheers for the insurance company to keep his premiums. Nonetheless, protect your assets and purchase as much insurance as you need and can afford. Health insurance premiums are expensive and eat up too much of the average family's income, but don't fret (it won't help the situation), usually there are options - be creative to develop one that works for you. Do what it takes to protect you and your family; realize, it might require a significant sacrifice. That's OK, make the sacrifice, do what needs to be done, and work to make things better. As Americans, we have a history of doing just that.

6.2: Strategies – How much, at what price, from whom?

Purchasing insurance should be strategic in the sense that you should have a plan. The primary goal, though, is not to reduce premiums – that is easy; simply, the more risk you are willing to keep (higher shared costs/higher deductible), the less your monthly premium. Your strategic plan should be focused on managing as much risk as necessary to meet your goals and protect your assets. Everyone's situations and personalities are different, so do what works best for you. I really don't think there is a cookie-cutter approach that overlays perfectly for a broad audience. Customizing a risk management plan that meets your needs will require rolling up your sleeves and investing some time.

How much? Usually this refers to how much coverage do you need. If you have a car that is worth $1,000, it would be hard to justify comprehensive and collision insurance coverage. Liability is all you probably need. On the opposite end of the spectrum, if you just bought a $40,000 dually it would be nonsensical not to have <u>full coverage</u> on the truck. What about life insurance, how much do you need?

Again, very individualized, but at least purchase a policy with a death benefit large enough for the beneficiary to pay off all of your outstanding obligations (debts, medical bills, funeral expenses, etc.) and deposit a little in savings. That would be a minimum; you don't want to leave your family with liabilities. If you are a relatively healthy, normal 20-something, you can purchase significant amounts (hundreds of thousands of dollars) of term life insurance for $15-$20 per month.

Insurance is all about off-loading risk for a price. If you don't share any of the risk with a counter party, you are in essence self-insuring. That is the cheapest way to go because it doesn't cost you anything in premiums, but you cover any and all losses personally. No losses? You are substantially ahead. One major incident and you may go bankrupt. Kind of a gamble, but that's the game. If you off-load all of the risk to a counter party, you can sleep well at night. Regardless of what happens (as long as it is completely covered per the contract – make sure and read the footnotes), you will be made whole by the counter party. Your insurance partner doesn't accept all of that risk for free though; he charges an annual premium that reflects his risk of loss. That premium can be financially painful to your checkbook. Between self-insuring and paying someone else to carry all of the risk is where most insurance carriers and customers meet. By risk sharing, customers accept risk of loss up to a certain financial level, then, the carrier assumes the rest. Risk-sharing policies can be customized for almost any situation and are only limited, usually, by government stricture or price.

So, at what price do you self-insure, share risk, or transfer all of the risk, and to whom? That is up to you and your insurance carrier of choice. All carriers have knowledgeable reps and agents willing to help you flesh these things out. I would suggest not taking any one person's advice unless you fully trust them and are completely comfortable with their insurance acumen. Talk to multiple reps and agents at numerous companies and determine which policy meets your needs best.

Yes, it takes time and effort. Read policy proposals. Ask a lot of questions. Try and understand everything you need to know to make a good decision. The insurance industry has innumerable reps/agents who are seasoned professionals. Of course some are lazy, unethical, and "graduated" last in their class, just like in any industry, but most want to do a good job for their customer. If you happen to come across a bad one, get rid of him. There are more than enough good ones who would love to have your business. It does take time, but so what, that's what mature, responsible people do. They take the time to become informed consumers. Again, don't be one of those people who will spend hundreds of hours playing computer games while refusing to spend half that much time learning, researching, and discussing insurance protection for your hard-earned assets.

Summary – Your insurance policies should be customized to meet your particular needs at a comfortable risk level, and at a price you can afford. To manage all of your risks prudently, you may have to make serious sacrifices; do so because that's what responsible adults do. Take the time required to research, ask questions, and learn about policy proposals before you make a purchase. Give up video games and TV, if necessary, to find the time to become an informed consumer.

6.3: Risk Management - Catch 22: Protecting assets may put you in the poorhouse; not protecting assets may put you in the poorhouse; go into the insurance business......

We pretty much made this case previously. Insurance is a necessary evil; it's a pain, but it is prudent. Arming yourself with knowledge and surrounding yourself with really sharp insurance reps/agents is necessary to purchase the most optimal insurance products – the right level of risk-sharing for your needs at the best available/most affordable price. You can't really do anymore than that, except.....

.....you could go into the insurance business. Become an agent, own a brokerage, own stock in a carrier.....this is the only way I know of to recycle some of your insurance premiums. If you don't want to get into the insurance industry as an agent, a broker or an owner, you are relegated to the optimize-your-purchase strategy above. Work hard, do your research, spend time asking questions and meeting with reps/agents, then bite the bullet, get out your checkbook, put a smile on your face, and root for the insurance company to win; it's in your best interest to do so.

Summary – If you can't beat them, join them. If you don't want to join them, smile, write a check, and then root for 'em.

Typical Insurance Policies:

Health (Medical/Dental/Eye-care)
Life (Term/Permanent)
Disability (Short-term and/or Long-term)
Automobile (Liability, Comprehensive/Collision)
Homeowners (structure and belongings) or Renters (belongings)
>(All of a dwelling policy is important, but make sure you are aware of any nuance to the deductible or limits on coverage re: fire, flooding, and wind damage.)

Umbrella (Additional Liability)

DISCUSSION 7: CONCLUSION

What is the impetus of this discussion? I want to encourage you to take control of your life, your destiny, and embrace all of the opportunities that are afforded to you.

Recap:

Understand freedom. Develop a plan that moves you toward financial independence.

Take advantage of 21st century educational opportunities. Learning new skill sets is only a click away. Never has it been so convenient to improve your lot.

Never spend more than you earn. Never finance (pay interest on) depreciating assets. And never, ever finance consumption!

Save, save, save.....build up a reserve fund, an emergency savings fund and start your retirement fund NOW!

Starting out, invest your retirement funds into separate classes of assets via mutual funds. This diversification strategy will reduce your systematic and unsystematic risks, concurrently. Be disciplined, be diligent, and allow time and compounding interest to be assets, which means start investing asap.

One big part of the American Dream is to own a home. Whether you buy or build, becoming a landowner has a positive impact on you personally, and it is a positive for society at large. Learn from the mistakes of others and take advantage of the opportunities that are before you. Work hard, take your shots (and keep shooting), and, when it is right for you, pull the trigger on home ownership. But regardless of whether you are an owner or a renter, begin building relationships and creating memories now, at your home, in your community. Prioritize what really matters in life, and understand that material things are just that, things. Relationships are at the core of humanity.

Insurance is a necessary evil.....buy what you need to protect you and your family (and all assets that need protected), but don't be a lazy consumer. Ask questions and learn - talk to multiple reps/agents and carriers. Get the optimal policies for your situation.

"Live Free Or Die;..." – How audacious a motto, but it couldn't be any more spot on. You should be protective of your individual liberty. You should be willing to fight whenever necessary to preserve freedom for you and your progeny. It's not just an historical textbook concept; freedom is inherent to the nature of man and should be respected and defended, always. "...Death Is Not The Worst Of Evils."

Plan:

Define success on your terms. Don't allow yourself to be boxed into someone else's idea of success. Otherwise, you may not be committed to a plan because the end result may not really be what you want. Take ownership of your ideas, your dreams, your plans. Really, seriously, look deep inside yourself and figure out what you want to accomplish in life. It goes so much faster than you can imagine. You do not have a lot of time to dink around. Every day you let slip by puts you another day away from reaching your full potential, and it eliminates a day you could have used to positively impact your world.

If you have no "grande plans" in mind, you still haven't gotten the drift of this discussion. I would encourage you to read it again, but this time share some reflection time after each discussion with a mentor.

Hopefully you are not selfish and shallow, nor mean and nasty. If so, I hope you meet someone who makes a positive difference in your life. Turn that negative energy around and you will enjoy your success so much more. If you really have no desire to accomplish anything – lazy and apathetic - and just want to sit in front of your TV until your time ends, then best of luck, though I would discourage that attitude. I hope you live a calm, peaceful and happy life, but it is sad to think what you could have accomplished with a little gumption. You do have unique capabilities, whether you recognize them or not. I challenge you to find inspiration – find your why and you'll figure out the how.

If you are positive, motivated, energetic, and excited about your life, then set some goals and get after it! You're the target of this book. Don't wait for the right time; don't wait for other people. Now is the time, and you are the right person. Whatever your "grande plan" – attack it!

Set Goals. Write your goals down on a piece of paper. Develop a strategic plan that provides a pathway to success. Within that strategic plan, implement daily building blocks that continually move you down that path. Measure your results. Assess them. Alter them when necessary. Continually evaluate your overall plan and make sure it is on track. There are scores of different methodologies available to consult as you create your plan and tactics. Resources are plentiful (Search "Goal-setting plans"). Find something that works for you and commit to it.

Broadly, I would say make sure you set clear and definable goals that motivate you. Remember, if you know the why, you will figure out the how. Develop a plan that makes sense. Work the plan. If upon regular assessment you realize the plan isn't working, don't be afraid to alter the plan. It happens all the time – on the field of battle, on the playing field, in the Boardroom. If you view each setback as a failure, you should redefine failure; mostly, it is an opportunity to learn and improve. (Is your cup half empty or half full?)

Conclusion:

Lastly, be open to a mentor. Listen, learn, and apply. Be accountable. Develop deep and lasting relationships. Then, become a mentor yourself. Invest in other people's lives. There is no way to overstate how important relationships are to your overall well-being. Investing in people takes time and energy; fortunately, at your age it is reasonable to assume you have both.

Life is short, so start now and make the most of it, and do it the right way! When your journey is complete I hope you can say, "I have fought the good fight, I have finished the race, I have kept the faith."

"And so I close by quoting the words of an old Negro slave preacher who didn't quite have his grammar right, but uttered words of great and profound significance:

> 'Lord, we ain't what we oughta be;
> We ain't what we wanna be;
> We ain't what we're gonna be;
> But thank God we ain't what we was.'"

Excerpt of Rev. Dr. Martin Luther King, Jr.
"Remaining Awake Through a Great Revolution"
Commencement Address for Oberlin College
June 1965, Oberlin Ohio

Please visit <u>4t Nox U</u>, use the resources, and keep in touch. We welcome feedback and periodic updates on your progress. God Bless.

DEBT WARNING:

It is better to be out of than in, but if you must be in debt make sure it is manageable. Unfortunately, even if your personal balance sheet has no debt on it, you're still on the hook for an obscene amount of money. $16,000,000,000,000.00 (U.S. National Debt) divided by 300 million people equals **$53,333.33** of debt for every single person in the United States. (The median household income is just over $50,000 per year.) Per capita income in 2010 was $27,334, meaning the government would need to confiscate 100% of everyone's income for two years to pay our **current** national debt, but only half of households in the country pay federal income taxes, i.e., your tax burden far exceeds $53,333.

(FYI: Most of the federal government's revenue comes from income taxes - 47.4% personal income / 7.9% corporate income [Table 2.2].)

To add insult to injury, and liabilities to your "tax bill", we have tens of trillions of dollars in unfunded obligations (not included in the current debt figure above), and we have run a ~$1.1T annual budget deficit (on average - Table 1.1) for the last four years – **that's T for Trillion, annually!** According to a USA TODAY analysis, the total national debt tab at the end of 2010 stood at **$61.6 Trillion - $528,000 per household** - and is growing unsustainably. Essentially, national leaders are playing roulette with our future; I neither have the risk tolerance for this gamble nor the confidence that they will quit choosing to double down on red, which has landed us where we are at, and avert a debt/monetary crisis. This is a very serious issue that needs addressed immediately.

Understand that the expanding debt bomb, while a symptom of a deeper cause, has now become the primary threat to your future happiness and well being, to your unalienable rights, to your children's and grandchildren's pursuit of freedom. Invasion by an external/foreign army is a peripheral national threat at best; an internal issue like a march toward socio-economic and geographic disunity is serious yet slow-dripping; but, the causes of excessive deficit spending leading to unsustainable debt, regardless of their *necessity*, and the structural budget imbalances that lead to gross unfunded obligations have created a bureaucratic, downhill snowball that will be hard to stop from crashing and collapsing. Piteously, there is no political will to do so as providing bread and games seem to retain one's position, and better to maintain power in a state which is in decline (by "going along to get along", by being a "team player", and by not voting responsibly or even conscionably) than to be without in any state – they, politicos, know the snowball won't easily be slowed down, much less be stopped.

Not that disaster is assured or the republic will fail. America can turn the tide and avoid a catastrophic implosion before it is too late, but the clock is ticking, and the longer we wait the direr the situation - There is a time limit. If we do not start now to get our house in order (eliminate deficit spending, begin chipping away at our national debt, and reform/reduce the growth of and extend the time of unfunded liabilities so future obligations become funded), and demand political courage from those wanting to "serve" their constituents, eventually we'll pay a heavy price for profligacy and apathy - monetary inflation, lower standard of living, confiscatory taxes, loss of individual liberty, a weakened defense apparatus, a declining empirical influence, etc.

Irresponsibility has brought us to this point. It took us 200 years to run up $1T in debt.....and 30 years to add the next $15T (Table 7.1). We have little room for excess, be it the welfare state, the military-industrial complex, corporate bailouts, or additional debt for "stimulus". Your generation does not have the convenience of passing the buck. All producers of your era, and the next (and possibly the next), will bear the brunt of the necessary fiscal and financial recalibration, or suffer the consequences of inaction. It will take a lot of hard work and sacrifice, but you don't have much of a choice. Currently, the financial path we are on is one of ruin. That is not an alarmist statement; it is just an observable, logical fact. America must get on a sustainable fiscal path very soon – the results of not doing so will dwarf the costs (sacrifice).

The reality is - You have been swindled, on a large scale; don't do the same to your posterity.

"And I sincerely believe, with you, that banking establishments are more dangerous than standing armies; and that the principle of spending money to be paid by posterity, under the name of funding, is but swindling futurity on a large scale."

(Thomas Jefferson to John Taylor, 1816)

"And our right may be doubted of mortgaging posterity for the expenses of a war in which they will have a right to say their interests were not concerned. It is incumbent on every generation to pay its own debts as it goes. A principle which, if acted on, would save one half the wars of the world."

(Thomas Jefferson to A.L.C. Destutt de Tracy, 1820)

"Personal debt levels are elevated, which is unstable, but our public debt is becoming ridiculously unsustainable and it will result either in a financial crisis, a confiscatory tax regime, civil unrest and foreign war, or all of the above. It is a serious problem."

(Unknown, overheard by happenstance in a recent coffee house conversation, 2012)

APPENDIX A
Freedom Indicator (FI)

The Freedom Indicator (FI) is a simple calculation, but more than that it is an idea that redefines the way people think about capital and their personal finances.

Most people would say that a Vice President making $200,000 per year is financially successful. Maybe, maybe not – better stated, he makes a good income. If he is spending $250,000 every year, running an annual $50,000 budget deficit, then it would not be accurate to say he is financially successful. Also, more to the point of the FI, he must go to work each day to earn the $200,000. If he does not go to work, it is safe to say his employer will not feel obliged to pay him this generous salary. While not an indentured servant by any means, he is shackled, in a sense, by golden handcuffs. Obviously he has a lifestyle that exceeds his income already; he is not free to do other things unless there is a substantial change in his budget, OR, unless he has enough assets to generate the income necessary to support his standard of living (the essence of the Freedom Indicator).

To be truly free you need to build a personal balance sheet fortress - your money needs to work for you and not the other way around. To illustrate this idea I will put forth a couple of balance sheet examples that show what this type of freedom looks like. As you will notice in each example, I am assuming you will need $50,000 in annual income to cover your expenses and that you paid off all personal debt.

Example 1: Investment Portfolio

Assets:

Investment accounts (aggregate) -	$1,000,000
Home -	$200,000
Investment Real Estate -	$0
Private Pension -	$0
Other -	$0

Liabilities:

Mortgage -	$0
Personal Loans -	$0
Investment Loans -	$0
Other -	$0

Net Worth:

Total -	$1,200,000

If your $1,000,000 investment account (dividend paying stocks, preferred stocks, corporate bonds, and government bills/notes) earns 5% per year on average, you will earn $50,000 per year. If your annual expenses are $50,000 per year, you are effectively financially free. Assuming you are not Social Security eligible and the investment account is your only source of income, you may not be prepared for emergencies or future underperformance (earning less than 5%), but you have at least gotten to a point where your money is working for you at a level that does not force you to work anymore to meet your needs. You are now free to pursue whatever you desire as long as you can keep your annual expenses under $50,000.

Example 2: Real Estate Portfolio

Assets:

Investment accounts (aggregate) -	$100,000
Home -	$200,000
Investment Real Estate -	$500,000
Private Pension -	(monthly income for life)
Other -	$0

Liabilities:

Mortgage -	$0
Personal Loans -	$0
Investment Loans -	$300,000
Other -	$0

Net Worth:

Total -	$500,000

If your investment accounts earn 5% per year on average, you will only be earning $5,000 per year. You still need $45,000 per year in earnings to cover your annual expenses. Assume that your net operating income (income after all insurance, taxes, maintenance, loan payment, etc.) of the real estate portfolio is 5%. $500,000 x 5% = $25,000. By adding the $25,000 real estate income to your $5,000 investment income, you end up with $30,000 in annual income. You need an extra $20,000 per year coming from somewhere. Thankfully your private pension pays you $1,500 per month ($18,000/year) for life. In this example, you end up earning $2,000 ($167/month) less than you spend each year. This is manageable as you are likely able to either reduce your expenses (maybe discontinue the HD 1,000 channel digital cable subscription) or increase your net operating income (to 5.4%) to make up the difference. Of course, once your real estate loan is paid off your net operating income will increase by the same amount (cash flow transfers from the bank to you), all things being equal. And, once you are eligible to receive Social Security benefits your income will increase accordingly.

This example has a different composition of assets than the first one, and the net worth is less than half as much, but it still does the job with regard to the FI. Example 2 sets you just as free as Example 1, which is the goal.

Example 3: Pension Portfolio

Assets:

Investment accounts (aggregate) -	$0
Home -	$200,000
Investment Real Estate -	$0
Private Pension -	(monthly income for life)
Other – Social Security	(monthly income for life)

Liabilities:

Mortgage -	$0
Personal Loans -	$0
Investment Loans -	$0
Other -	$0

Net Worth:

Total -	$200,000

Obviously in this example the balance sheet is not yet a fortress. There are no assets beyond the private and public pension plans that can be used to generate income. If the private pension pays $1,500 per month, and the Social Security benefit is $1,500 per month ($18,000 + $18,000 = $36,000 per year), one would end up $14,000 short of covering the assumed annual expenses. One could either work for the additional $14,000 per year (trading freedom for wages) or reduce one's standard of living/monthly expenses to meet the income level. Limited assets limit options.

Begin now to build assets which can be used to generate future income – get your money working for you as soon as possible!

So that you don't get the wrong idea – There is nothing wrong with trading your time for money, i.e., working for wages. It is how most people will build their personal balance sheet fortress. Work should be praised and encouraged. As long as you are willing and able to contribute there is no reason you shouldn't. The point of the FI is to promote capital investment with your surplus income. Instead of spending money on non-income producing, depreciating assets, or needless consumption, get in the habit of investing your money in income-producing, appreciating assets.

We live in a capitalist system yet we grow up with a misunderstanding of capital. Capital should be invested in productive assets. Consumption is fine and necessary (otherwise no one would buy your products or services), but "consumerism" (spending [worse yet – financing on a credit card] haphazardly on stuff to fill a storage facility, garage or attic) is not the way to build a personal balance sheet fortress.

The FI is a simple framework to be used to determine your number (set a goal) and develop a corresponding plan to achieve your objective. Hopefully it encourages you to invest your capital strategically and productively.

Pertinent FI questions?

How much income do you need to cover your expenses (plus emergencies and savings)?

How many assets do you need (and what type) to produce the required income?

When do you want to become financially free (i.e., when your money works for you to the point that it covers your monthly expenses versus you trading your time for wages)?

What are you doing today to reach your "magic" FI number?

Develop a plan, deploy your capital, compound your earnings, and allow time to be an asset and not a liability. Generate surplus income (via your budget) and invest that capital in appreciating and income-producing assets. Build your fortress!

APPENDIX B

	January	February	March	April	May	June	July	August	September	October	November	December	Totals	% Wages
Revenue:														
Net Wages	2300	2300	2300	2300	2300	2300	2300	2300	2300	2300	2300	2300	27600	100.00
Expenses:														
Home Ownership														
Mortgage	350	350	350	350	350	350	350	350	350	350	350	350	4200	15.22
House Insurance	0	0	0	0	0	0	0	0	0	0	0	0	0	0.00
Property Taxes	0	0	0	0	0	0	0	0	0	0	0	0	0	0.00
Home Maintenance														
Home Repairs	0	0	0	0	0	0	0	0	0	0	0	0	0	0.00
Utilities														
Electric Bill	125	125	125	125	125	125	125	125	125	125	125	125	1500	5.43
Natural Gas Bill	20	20	20	20	20	20	20	20	20	20	20	20	240	0.87
Cable	45	45	45	45	45	45	45	45	45	45	45	45	540	1.96
Internet Connectivity	35	35	35	35	35	35	35	35	35	35	35	35	420	1.52
Water Bill	25	25	25	25	25	25	25	25	25	25	25	25	300	1.09
Trash Pick-Up	15	15	15	15	15	15	15	15	15	15	15	15	180	0.65
Telephone	25	25	25	25	25	25	25	25	25	25	25	25	300	1.09
Automobiles														
Car(s)	250	250	250	250	250	250	250	250	250	250	250	250	3000	10.87
Car(s) Insurance	150	150	150	150	150	150	150	150	150	150	150	150	1800	6.52
Gas	150	150	150	150	150	150	150	150	150	150	150	150	1800	6.52
Car Maintenance	50	50	50	50	50	50	50	50	50	50	50	50	600	2.17
Medical														

													Total	%
Health Insurance	200	200	200	200	200	200	200	200	200	200	200	200	2400	8.70
Medical Expenses	100	100	100	100	100	100	100	100	100	100	100	100	1200	4.35
Life Insurance	15	15	15	15	15	15	15	15	15	15	15	15	180	0.65
Household Items														
Food	150	150	150	150	150	150	150	150	150	150	150	150	1800	6.52
Cleaning/Toiletries	25	25	25	25	25	25	25	25	25	25	25	25	300	1.09
Personal														
Clothes	50	50	50	50	50	50	50	50	50	50	50	50	600	2.17
Cell Phone	50	50	50	50	50	50	50	50	50	50	50	50	600	2.17
Mag/News Subscriptions	25	25	25	25	25	25	25	25	25	25	25	25	300	1.09
Nights Out/Dating	100	100	100	100	100	100	100	100	100	100	100	100	1200	4.35
Debt														
Credit Cards	50	50	50	50	50	50	50	50	50	50	50	50	600	2.17
School Loans	0	0	0	0	0	0	0	0	0	0	0	0	0	0.00
Miscellaneous														
Misc. - Fun Items	50	50	50	50	50	50	50	50	50	50	50	50	600	2.17
Vacation	50	50	50	50	50	50	50	50	50	50	50	50	600	2.17
Taxes	0	0	0	0	0	0	0	0	0	0	0	0	0	0.00
Balance	195	195	195	195	195	195	195	195	195	195	195	195	2340	
Savings														
Reserve Account	50	50	50	50	50	50	50	50	50	50	50	50	600	2.17
Down Payment	0	0	0	0	0	0	0	0	0	0	0	0	0	0.00
Retirement	50	50	50	50	50	50	50	50	50	50	50	50	600	2.17
Balance	95	95	95	95	95	95	95	95	95	95	95	95	1140	

Gifts	50	50	50	50	50	50	50	50	50	50	50	600	2.17
Balance	45	45	45	45	45	45	45	45	45	45	45	540	540
Total	45	90	135	180	225	270	315	360	405	450	495	540	540	98.04

APPENDIX C-1

Single Sum of $1 Future Value Table

$(1+i)^n$

n	0.50%	1%	1.50%	2%	3%	4%	5%	6%	7%	8%	9%	10%	11%	12%	13%	14%	15%	16%	17%	18%	19%	20%
1	1.005	1.01	1.015	1.02	1.03	1.04	1.05	1.06	1.07	1.08	1.09	1.1	1.11	1.12	1.13	1.14	1.15	1.16	1.17	1.18	1.19	1.2
2	1.01	1.02	1.03	1.04	1.061	1.082	1.103	1.124	1.145	1.166	1.188	1.21	1.232	1.254	1.277	1.3	1.323	1.346	1.369	1.392	1.416	1.44
3	1.015	1.03	1.046	1.061	1.093	1.125	1.158	1.191	1.225	1.26	1.295	1.331	1.368	1.405	1.443	1.482	1.521	1.561	1.602	1.643	1.685	1.728
4	1.02	1.041	1.061	1.082	1.126	1.17	1.216	1.262	1.311	1.36	1.412	1.464	1.518	1.574	1.63	1.689	1.749	1.811	1.874	1.939	2.005	2.074
5	1.025	1.051	1.077	1.104	1.159	1.217	1.276	1.338	1.403	1.469	1.539	1.611	1.685	1.762	1.842	1.925	2.011	2.1	2.192	2.288	2.386	2.488
6	1.03	1.062	1.093	1.126	1.194	1.265	1.34	1.419	1.501	1.587	1.677	1.772	1.87	1.974	2.082	2.195	2.313	2.436	2.565	2.7	2.84	2.986
7	1.036	1.072	1.11	1.149	1.23	1.316	1.407	1.504	1.606	1.714	1.828	1.949	2.076	2.211	2.353	2.502	2.66	2.826	3.001	3.185	3.379	3.583
8	1.041	1.083	1.126	1.172	1.267	1.369	1.477	1.594	1.718	1.851	1.993	2.144	2.305	2.476	2.658	2.853	3.059	3.278	3.511	3.759	4.021	4.3
9	1.046	1.094	1.143	1.195	1.305	1.423	1.551	1.689	1.838	1.999	2.172	2.358	2.558	2.773	3.004	3.252	3.518	3.803	4.108	4.435	4.785	5.16
10	1.051	1.105	1.161	1.219	1.344	1.48	1.629	1.791	1.967	2.159	2.367	2.594	2.839	3.106	3.395	3.707	4.046	4.411	4.807	5.234	5.695	6.192
11	1.056	1.116	1.178	1.243	1.384	1.539	1.71	1.898	2.105	2.332	2.58	2.853	3.152	3.479	3.836	4.226	4.652	5.117	5.624	6.176	6.777	7.43
12	1.062	1.127	1.196	1.268	1.426	1.601	1.796	2.012	2.252	2.518	2.813	3.138	3.498	3.896	4.335	4.818	5.35	5.936	6.58	7.288	8.064	8.916
13	1.067	1.138	1.214	1.294	1.469	1.665	1.886	2.133	2.41	2.72	3.066	3.452	3.883	4.363	4.898	5.492	6.153	6.886	7.699	8.599	9.596	10.699
14	1.072	1.149	1.232	1.319	1.513	1.732	1.98	2.261	2.579	2.937	3.342	3.797	4.31	4.887	5.535	6.261	7.076	7.988	9.007	10.147	11.42	12.839
15	1.078	1.161	1.25	1.346	1.558	1.801	2.079	2.397	2.759	3.172	3.642	4.177	4.785	5.474	6.254	7.138	8.137	9.266	10.539	11.974	13.59	15.407
16	1.083	1.173	1.269	1.373	1.605	1.873	2.183	2.54	2.952	3.426	3.97	4.595	5.311	6.13	7.067	8.137	9.358	10.748	12.33	14.129	16.172	18.488
17	1.088	1.184	1.288	1.4	1.653	1.948	2.292	2.693	3.159	3.7	4.328	5.054	5.895	6.866	7.986	9.276	10.761	12.468	14.426	16.672	19.244	22.186
18	1.094	1.196	1.307	1.428	1.702	2.026	2.407	2.854	3.38	3.996	4.717	5.56	6.544	7.69	9.024	10.575	12.375	14.463	16.879	19.673	22.901	26.623
19	1.099	1.208	1.327	1.457	1.754	2.107	2.527	3.026	3.617	4.316	5.142	6.116	7.263	8.613	10.197	12.056	14.232	16.777	19.748	23.214	27.252	31.948
20	1.105	1.22	1.347	1.486	1.806	2.191	2.653	3.207	3.87	4.661	5.604	6.727	8.062	9.646	11.523	13.743	16.367	19.461	23.106	27.393	32.429	38.338
21	1.11	1.232	1.367	1.516	1.86	2.279	2.786	3.4	4.141	5.034	6.109	7.4	8.949	10.804	13.021	15.668	18.822	22.574	27.034	32.324	38.591	46.005
22	1.116	1.245	1.388	1.546	1.916	2.37	2.925	3.604	4.43	5.437	6.659	8.14	9.934	12.1	14.714	17.861	21.645	26.186	31.629	38.142	45.923	55.206
23	1.122	1.257	1.408	1.577	1.974	2.465	3.072	3.82	4.741	5.871	7.258	8.954	11.026	13.552	16.627	20.362	24.891	30.376	37.006	45.008	54.649	66.247

	0.50%	1%	1.50%	2%	3%	4%	5%	6%	7%	8%	9%	10%	11%	12%	13%	14%	15%	16%	17%	18%	19%	20%
24	1.127	1.27	1.43	1.606	2.033	2.563	3.225	4.049	5.072	6.341	7.911	9.85	12.239	15.179	18.788	23.212	28.625	35.236	43.297	53.109	65.032	79.497
25	1.133	1.282	1.451	1.641	2.094	2.666	3.386	4.292	5.427	6.848	8.623	10.835	13.585	17	21.231	26.462	32.919	40.874	50.658	62.669	77.388	95.396
26	1.138	1.295	1.473	1.673	2.157	2.772	3.556	4.549	5.807	7.396	9.399	11.918	15.08	19.04	23.991	30.167	37.857	47.414	59.27	73.949	92.092	114.475
27	1.144	1.308	1.495	1.707	2.221	2.883	3.733	4.822	6.214	7.988	10.245	13.11	16.739	21.325	27.109	34.39	43.535	55	69.345	87.26	109.589	137.371
28	1.15	1.321	1.517	1.741	2.288	2.999	3.92	5.112	6.649	8.627	11.167	14.421	18.58	23.884	30.633	39.204	50.066	63.8	81.134	102.967	130.41	164.845
29	1.156	1.335	1.54	1.776	2.357	3.119	4.116	5.418	7.114	9.317	12.172	15.863	20.624	26.75	34.616	44.693	57.575	74.009	94.927	121.501	155.189	197.814
30	1.161	1.348	1.563	1.811	2.427	3.243	4.322	5.743	7.612	10.063	13.268	17.449	22.892	29.96	39.116	50.95	66.212	85.85	111.065	143.371	184.675	237.376
31	1.167	1.361	1.587	1.848	2.5	3.373	4.538	6.088	8.145	10.868	14.462	19.194	25.41	33.555	44.201	58.083	76.144	99.586	129.946	169.177	219.764	284.852
32	1.173	1.375	1.61	1.885	2.575	3.508	4.765	6.453	8.715	11.737	15.763	21.114	28.206	37.582	49.947	66.215	87.565	115.52	152.036	199.629	261.519	341.822
33	1.179	1.389	1.634	1.922	2.652	3.648	5.003	6.841	9.325	12.676	17.182	23.225	31.308	42.092	56.44	75.485	100.7	134.003	177.883	235.563	311.207	410.186
34	1.185	1.403	1.659	1.961	2.732	3.794	5.253	7.251	9.978	13.69	18.728	25.548	34.752	47.143	63.777	86.053	115.805	155.443	208.123	277.964	370.337	492.224
35	1.191	1.417	1.684	2	2.814	3.946	5.516	7.686	10.677	14.785	20.414	28.102	38.575	52.8	72.069	98.1	133.176	180.314	243.503	327.997	440.701	590.668
36	1.197	1.431	1.709	2.04	2.898	4.104	5.792	8.147	11.424	15.968	22.251	30.913	42.818	59.136	81.437	111.834	153.152	209.164	284.899	387.037	524.434	708.802
37	1.203	1.445	1.735	2.081	2.985	4.268	6.081	8.636	12.224	17.246	24.254	34.004	47.528	66.232	92.024	127.491	176.125	242.631	333.332	456.703	624.076	850.562
38	1.209	1.46	1.761	2.122	3.075	4.439	6.385	9.154	13.079	18.625	26.437	37.404	52.756	74.18	103.987	145.34	202.543	281.452	389.998	538.91	742.651	1020.675
39	1.215	1.474	1.787	2.165	3.167	4.616	6.705	9.704	13.995	20.115	28.816	41.145	58.559	83.081	117.506	165.687	232.925	326.484	456.298	635.914	883.754	1224.81
40	1.221	1.489	1.814	2.208	3.262	4.801	7.04	10.286	14.974	21.725	31.409	45.259	65.001	93.051	132.782	188.884	267.864	378.721	533.869	750.378	1051.668	1469.772
41	1.227	1.504	1.841	2.252	3.36	4.993	7.392	10.903	16.023	23.462	34.236	49.785	72.151	104.217	150.043	215.327	308.043	439.317	624.626	885.446	1251.484	1763.726
42	1.233	1.519	1.869	2.297	3.461	5.193	7.762	11.557	17.144	25.339	37.318	54.764	80.088	116.723	169.549	245.473	354.25	509.607	730.813	1044.827	1489.266	2116.471
43	1.239	1.534	1.897	2.343	3.565	5.4	8.15	12.25	18.344	27.367	40.676	60.24	88.897	130.73	191.59	279.839	407.387	591.144	855.051	1232.896	1772.227	2539.765
44	1.245	1.549	1.925	2.39	3.671	5.617	8.557	12.985	19.628	29.556	44.337	66.264	98.676	146.418	216.497	319.017	468.495	685.727	1000.41	1454.817	2108.95	3047.718
45	1.252	1.565	1.954	2.438	3.782	5.841	8.985	13.765	21.002	31.92	48.327	72.89	109.53	163.988	244.641	363.679	538.769	795.444	1170.479	1716.684	2509.651	3657.262
46	1.258	1.58	1.984	2.487	3.895	6.075	9.434	14.59	22.473	34.474	52.677	80.18	121.579	183.666	276.445	414.594	619.585	922.715	1369.461	2025.687	2986.484	4388.714
47	1.264	1.596	2.013	2.536	4.012	6.318	9.906	15.466	24.046	37.232	57.418	88.197	134.952	205.706	312.383	472.637	712.522	1070.349	1602.269	2390.311	3553.916	5266.457
48	1.27	1.612	2.043	2.587	4.132	6.571	10.401	16.394	25.729	40.211	62.585	97.017	149.797	230.391	352.992	538.807	819.401	1241.605	1874.655	2820.567	4229.16	6319.749
49	1.277	1.628	2.074	2.639	4.256	6.833	10.921	17.378	27.53	43.427	68.218	106.719	166.275	258.038	398.881	614.239	942.311	1440.262	2193.346	3328.269	5032.701	7583.698
50	1.283	1.645	2.105	2.692	4.384	7.107	11.467	18.42	29.457	46.902	74.358	117.391	184.565	289.002	450.736	700.233	1083.657	1670.704	2566.215	3927.357	5988.914	9100.438
51	1.29	1.661	2.137	2.745	4.515	7.391	12.041	19.525	31.519	50.654	81.05	129.13	204.867	323.682	509.332	798.266	1246.206	1938.016	3002.472	4634.281	7126.808	10920.53
52	1.296	1.678	2.169	2.8	4.651	7.687	12.643	20.697	33.725	54.706	88.344	142.043	227.402	362.524	575.545	910.023	1433.137	2248.099	3512.892	5468.452	8480.901	13104.63

	0.50%	1%	1.50%	2%	3%	4%	5%	6%	7%	8%	9%	10%	11%	12%	13%	14%	15%	16%	17%	18%	19%	20%
53	1.303	1.694	2.201	2.856	4.79	7.994	13.275	21.939	36.066	59.083	96.295	156.247	252.417	406.027	650.366	1037.426	1648.108	2607.795	4110.084	6452.773	10092.27	15725.56
54	1.309	1.711	2.234	2.913	4.934	8.314	13.939	23.255	38.612	63.809	104.962	171.872	280.182	454.751	734.913	1182.666	1895.324	3025.042	4808.798	7614.272	12009.8	18570.67
55	1.316	1.729	2.268	2.972	5.082	8.646	14.636	24.65	41.315	68.914	114.408	189.059	311.002	509.321	830.452	1348.239	2179.622	3509.049	5626.294	8984.841	14291.67	22644.8
56	1.322	1.746	2.302	3.031	5.235	8.992	15.367	26.129	44.207	74.427	124.705	207.965	345.213	570.439	938.41	1536.992	2506.566	4070.497	6582.764	10602.11	17007.08	27173.76
57	1.329	1.763	2.336	3.092	5.392	9.352	16.136	27.697	47.302	80.381	135.928	228.762	383.186	638.892	1060.404	1752.171	2882.55	4721.776	7701.833	12510.49	20238.43	32608.52
58	1.335	1.781	2.372	3.154	5.553	9.726	16.943	29.359	50.613	86.812	148.162	251.638	425.337	715.559	1198.256	1997.475	3314.933	5477.26	9011.145	14762.38	24083.73	39130.02
59	1.342	1.799	2.407	3.217	5.72	10.115	17.79	31.12	54.156	93.757	161.497	276.801	472.124	801.426	1354.03	2277.122	3812.173	6353.622	10543.04	17419.61	28659.64	46956.26
60	1.349	1.817	2.443	3.281	5.892	10.52	18.679	32.988	57.946	101.257	176.031	304.482	524.057	897.597	1530.053	2595.919	4383.999	7370.201	12335.36	20555.14	34104.97	56347.51
61	1.356	1.835	2.48	3.347	6.068	10.94	19.613	34.967	62.003	109.358	191.874	334.93	581.704	1005.309	1728.96	2959.347	5041.599	8549.434	14432.37	24255.07	40584.92	67617.02
62	1.362	1.853	2.517	3.414	6.25	11.378	20.594	37.065	66.343	118.106	209.145	368.423	645.691	1125.946	1953.725	3373.656	5797.808	9917.343	16885.87	23620.98	48296.05	81140.42
63	1.369	1.872	2.555	3.482	6.438	11.833	21.623	39.289	70.987	127.555	227.966	405.265	716.717	1261.059	2207.71	3845.968	6667.514	11504.12	19756.47	33772.75	574723	97368.51
64	1.376	1.89	2.593	3.551	6.631	12.306	22.705	41.646	75.956	137.759	248.483	445.792	795.556	1412.386	2494.712	4384.403	7667.641	13344.78	23115.07	39851.85	683922.04	116842.2
65	1.383	1.909	2.632	3.623	6.83	12.799	23.84	44.145	81.273	148.78	270.846	490.371	883.067	1581.872	2819.024	4998.22	8817.787	15479.94	27044.63	47025.18	81386.52	140210.6
66	1.39	1.928	2.672	3.695	7.035	13.311	25.032	46.794	86.962	160.682	295.222	539.408	980.204	1771.697	3185.498	5697.97	10140.46	17956.73	31642.22	55489.71	96849.96	168252.8
67	1.397	1.948	2.712	3.769	7.246	13.843	26.283	49.601	93.049	173.537	321.792	593.349	1088.027	1984.301	3599.612	6495.686	11661.52	20829.81	37021.39	65477.86	115251.5	201903.3
68	1.404	1.967	2.752	3.844	7.463	14.397	27.598	52.577	99.563	187.42	350.753	652.683	1207.71	2222.417	4067.562	7405.082	13410.75	24162.58	43315.03	77263.89	137149.2	242284
69	1.411	1.987	2.794	3.921	7.687	14.973	28.978	55.732	106.532	202.413	382.321	717.952	1340.558	2489.107	4596.345	8441.794	15422.37	28028.59	50678.58	91171.38	163207.6	290740.8
70	1.418	2.007	2.835	4	7.918	15.572	30.426	59.076	113.989	218.606	416.73	789.747	1488.019	2767.8	5193.87	9623.645	17735.72	32513.17	59293.94	107582.2	194217	348889
71	1.425	2.027	2.878	4.08	8.155	16.194	31.948	62.62	121.969	236.095	454.236	868.722	1651.701	3122.336	5869.073	10970.96	20396.08	37715.27	69373.91	126947	231118.3	418666.7
72	1.432	2.047	2.921	4.161	8.4	16.842	33.545	66.378	130.506	254.983	495.117	955.594	1833.388	3497.016	6632.052	12506.89	23455.49	43749.72	81167.48	149797.5	275030.7	503400.1
73	1.439	2.068	2.965	4.244	8.652	17.516	35.222	70.36	139.642	275.381	539.678	1051.153	2035.061	3916.658	7494.219	14257.85	26973.81	50749.67	94965.95	176761	327786.6	603980.1
74	1.446	2.088	3.009	4.329	8.912	18.217	36.984	74.582	149.417	297.412	588.249	1156.269	2258.918	4386.657	8468.467	16253.95	31019.89	58869.62	111110.2	208578	389471	723456.1
75	1.454	2.109	3.055	4.416	9.179	18.945	38.833	79.057	159.876	321.205	641.191	1271.895	2507.399	4913.056	9569.368	18529.51	33672.87	68298.76	129998.9	246122.1	463470.5	868147.4
76	1.461	2.13	3.1	4.504	9.454	19.703	40.774	83.8	171.067	346.901	698.898	1399.085	2783.213	5502.623	10813.39	21123.64	41023.8	79214.96	152098.7	290424	551529.9	1041777
77	1.468	2.152	3.147	4.594	9.738	20.491	42.813	88.828	183.042	374.653	761.799	1538.993	3089.366	6162.937	12219.13	24090.95	47177.37	91889.35	177955.5	342700.4	656320.6	1250132
78	1.476	2.173	3.194	4.686	10.03	21.311	44.954	94.158	195.855	404.625	830.361	1692.893	3429.196	6902.49	13807.61	27452.28	54253.97	106591.6	208207.9	404386.4	781021.5	1500159
79	1.483	2.195	3.242	4.78	10.331	22.163	47.201	99.808	209.565	436.995	905.093	1862.182	3806.408	7730.788	15602.6	31295.6	62392.07	123446.3	243603.3	477176	929415.6	1800190
80	1.49	2.217	3.291	4.875	10.641	23.05	49.561	105.796	224.234	471.955	986.552	2048.4	4225.113	8658.483	17630.94	35676.98	71750.88	143429.7	285015.8	563067.7	1106005	2160228

81	1.498	2.239	3.34	4.973	10.96	23.972	52.04	112.144	239.931	509.711	1075.341	2253.24	4689.875	9697.501	19922.96	40677.76	82513.51	166378.5	333468.5	664419.8	1316145	2592274
82	1.505	2.261	3.39	5.072	11.289	24.931	54.641	118.872	256.726	550.488	1172.122	2478.564	5205.761	10861.2	22512.95	46365.81	94890.54	192999	390198.1	784015.4	1566213	3110729
83	1.513	2.284	3.441	5.174	11.628	25.928	57.374	126.005	274.697	594.527	1277.613	2726.421	5778.395	12164.55	25439.63	52857.02	109124.1	228878.9	456485	925138.2	1863794	3732875
84	1.52	2.307	3.493	5.277	11.976	26.965	60.242	133.565	293.926	642.089	1392.598	2999.063	6414.019	13624.29	28746.78	60257	125492.7	259699.5	534087.5	1091663	2217914	4479450
85	1.528	2.33	3.545	5.383	12.336	28.044	63.254	141.579	314.5	693.456	1517.932	3298.969	7119.561	15259.21	32483.87	68692.98	144316.6	301251.4	624882.3	1288162	2639318	5375340
86	1.536	2.353	3.598	5.491	12.706	29.165	66.417	150.074	336.515	748.933	1654.546	3628.866	7902.712	17090.31	36706.77	78310	165944.1	349451.6	731112.3	1520032	3140788	6450408
87	1.543	2.377	3.652	5.6	13.087	30.332	69.738	159.078	360.071	808.848	1803.455	3991.753	8772.011	19141.15	41478.65	89273.4	190658.8	405363.9	855401.4	1793637	3737538	7740489
88	1.551	2.4	3.707	5.712	13.48	31.545	73.225	168.623	385.276	873.555	1965.766	4390.928	9736.932	21438.09	46870.67	101771.7	219487.6	470222.1	1000800	2116492	4447670	9288567
89	1.559	2.424	3.763	5.827	13.884	32.807	76.886	178.74	412.246	943.44	2142.685	4830.021	10807.99	24010.66	52964.09	116019.7	252410.7	545457.7	1170959	2497461	5292728	11146304
90	1.567	2.449	3.819	5.943	14.3	34.119	80.73	189.465	441.103	1018.915	2335.527	5313.023	11996.87	26891.93	59849.42	132262.5	290272.3	632730.9	1370022	2947004	6298346	13075565
91	1.574	2.473	3.876	6.062	14.729	35.484	84.767	200.832	471.98	1100.428	2545.724	5844.325	13316.53	30118.97	67629.84	150779.2	333813.2	733967.8	1602926	3477464	7495032	16050678
92	1.582	2.498	3.934	6.183	15.171	36.903	89.005	212.882	505.019	1188.463	2774.839	6428.757	14781.35	33733.24	76421.72	171888.3	383865.2	851402.7	1875423	4103408	8919088	19260814
93	1.59	2.523	3.993	6.307	15.627	38.38	93.455	225.656	540.37	1283.54	3024.575	7071.633	16407.3	37781.13	86356.54	195952.7	441467.9	987627.1	2194245	4842021	10613715	23112977
94	1.598	2.548	4.053	6.433	16.095	39.915	98.128	239.195	578.196	1386.223	3296.786	7778.796	18212.1	42314.98	97582.69	223396	507688.1	1145647	2567267	5713585	12630320	27735572
95	1.606	2.574	4.114	6.562	16.578	41.511	103.035	253.546	618.67	1497.121	3593.497	8556.676	20215.43	47392.78	110268.7	254660.1	583841.3	1328951	3003702	6742030	15030081	33282687
96	1.614	2.599	4.176	6.693	17.076	43.172	108.186	268.759	661.977	1616.89	3916.912	9412.344	22439.13	53079.91	124603.6	290312.5	671417.5	1541583	3514332	7955596	17885797	39939224
97	1.622	2.625	4.238	6.827	17.588	44.899	113.596	284.885	708.315	1746.241	4269.434	10353.58	24907.43	59449.5	140802.1	330956.2	772130.2	1788237	4111768	9387603	21284098	47927069
98	1.63	2.652	4.302	6.963	18.115	46.695	119.276	301.978	757.897	1885.941	4633.683	11388.94	27647.25	66583.14	159106.3	377290.1	887949.7	2074354	4810768	11077371	25328077	57512482
99	1.638	2.678	4.367	7.103	18.659	48.562	125.239	320.096	810.95	2036.816	5072.514	12527.83	30688.45	74573.45	179790.2	430110.7	1021142	2406251	5628599	13071298	30140412	69014979
100	1.647	2.705	4.432	7.245	19.219	50.505	131.501	339.302	867.716	2199.761	5529.041	13780.61	34064.18	83522.27	203162.9	490326.2	1174313	2791251	6585461	15424132	35667090	82817975

APPENDIX C-2

Ordinary Annuity of $1 Future Value Table

$$[(1+i)^n-1]/i$$

n	0.50%	1%	1.50%	2%	3%	4%	5%	6%	7%	8%	9%	10%	11%	12%	13%	14%	15%	16%	17%	18%	19%	20%
1	1	1	1	1	1	1	1	1	1	1	1	1	1	1	1	1	1	1	1	1	1	1
2	2.005	2.01	2.015	2.02	2.03	2.04	2.05	2.06	2.07	2.08	2.09	2.1	2.11	2.12	2.13	2.14	2.15	2.16	2.17	2.18	2.19	2.2
3	3.015	3.03	3.045	3.06	3.091	3.122	3.153	3.184	3.215	3.246	3.278	3.31	3.342	3.374	3.407	3.44	3.473	3.506	3.539	3.572	3.606	3.64
4	4.03	4.06	4.091	4.122	4.184	4.246	4.31	4.375	4.44	4.506	4.573	4.641	4.71	4.779	4.85	4.921	4.993	5.066	5.141	5.215	5.291	5.368
5	5.05	5.101	5.152	5.204	5.309	5.416	5.526	5.637	5.751	5.867	5.985	6.105	6.228	6.353	6.48	6.61	6.742	6.877	7.014	7.154	7.297	7.442
6	6.076	6.152	6.23	6.308	6.468	6.633	6.802	6.975	7.153	7.336	7.523	7.716	7.913	8.115	8.323	8.536	8.754	8.977	9.207	9.442	9.683	9.93
7	7.106	7.214	7.323	7.434	7.662	7.898	8.142	8.394	8.654	8.923	9.2	9.487	9.783	10.089	10.405	10.73	11.067	11.414	11.772	12.142	12.523	12.916
8	8.141	8.286	8.433	8.583	8.892	9.214	9.549	9.897	10.26	10.637	11.028	11.436	11.859	12.3	12.757	13.233	13.727	14.24	14.773	15.327	15.902	16.499
9	9.182	9.369	9.559	9.755	10.159	10.583	11.027	11.491	11.978	12.488	13.021	13.579	14.164	14.776	15.416	16.085	16.786	17.519	18.285	19.086	19.923	20.799
10	10.228	10.462	10.703	10.95	11.464	12.006	12.578	13.181	13.816	14.487	15.193	15.937	16.722	17.549	18.42	19.337	20.304	21.321	22.393	23.521	24.709	25.959
11	11.279	11.567	11.863	12.169	12.808	13.486	14.207	14.972	15.784	16.645	17.56	18.531	19.561	20.655	21.814	23.045	24.349	25.733	27.2	28.755	30.404	32.15
12	12.336	12.683	13.041	13.412	14.192	15.026	15.917	16.87	17.888	18.977	20.141	21.384	22.713	24.133	25.65	27.271	29.002	30.85	32.824	34.931	37.18	39.581
13	13.397	13.809	14.237	14.68	15.618	16.627	17.713	18.882	20.141	21.495	22.953	24.523	26.212	28.029	29.985	32.089	34.352	36.786	39.404	42.219	45.244	48.497
14	14.464	14.947	15.45	15.974	17.086	18.292	19.599	21.015	22.55	24.215	26.019	27.975	30.095	32.393	34.883	37.581	40.505	43.672	47.103	50.818	54.841	59.196
15	15.537	16.097	16.682	17.293	18.599	20.024	21.579	23.276	25.129	27.152	29.361	31.772	34.405	37.28	40.417	43.842	47.58	51.66	56.11	60.965	66.261	72.035
16	16.614	17.258	17.932	18.639	20.157	21.825	23.657	25.673	27.888	30.324	33.003	35.95	39.19	42.753	46.672	50.98	55.717	60.925	66.649	72.939	79.85	87.442
17	17.697	18.43	19.201	20.012	21.762	23.698	25.84	28.213	30.84	33.75	36.974	40.545	44.501	48.884	53.739	59.118	65.075	71.673	78.979	87.068	96.022	105.931
18	18.786	19.615	20.489	21.412	23.414	25.645	28.132	30.906	33.999	37.45	41.301	45.599	50.396	55.75	61.725	68.394	75.836	84.141	93.406	103.74	115.266	128.117
19	19.88	20.811	21.797	22.841	25.117	27.671	30.539	33.76	37.379	41.446	46.018	51.159	56.939	63.44	70.749	78.969	88.212	98.603	110.285	123.414	138.166	154.74
20	20.979	22.019	23.124	24.297	26.87	29.778	33.066	36.786	40.995	45.762	51.16	57.275	64.203	72.052	80.947	91.025	102.444	115.38	130.033	146.628	165.418	186.688
21	22.084	23.239	24.471	25.783	28.676	31.969	35.719	39.993	44.865	50.423	56.765	64.002	72.265	81.699	92.47	104.768	118.81	134.841	153.139	174.021	197.847	225.026
22	23.194	24.472	25.898	27.299	30.537	34.248	38.505	43.392	49.006	55.457	62.873	71.403	81.214	92.503	105.491	120.436	137.632	157.415	180.172	206.345	236.438	271.031

	0.50%	1%	1.50%	2%	3%	4%	5%	6%	7%	8%	9%	10%	11%	12%	13%	14%	15%	16%	17%	18%	19%	20%
23	24.31	25.716	27.225	28.845	32.453	36.618	41.43	46.996	53.436	60.893	69.532	79.543	91.148	104.603	120.205	138.297	159.276	183.601	211.801	244.487	282.362	326.237
24	25.432	26.973	28.634	30.422	34.426	39.083	44.502	50.816	58.177	66.765	76.79	88.497	102.174	118.155	136.831	158.659	184.168	213.978	248.808	289.494	337.01	392.484
25	26.559	28.243	30.063	32.03	36.459	41.646	47.727	54.865	63.249	73.106	84.701	98.347	114.413	133.334	155.62	181.871	212.793	249.214	292.105	342.603	402.042	471.981
26	27.692	29.526	31.514	33.671	38.553	44.312	51.113	59.156	68.676	79.954	93.324	109.182	127.999	150.334	176.85	208.333	245.712	290.088	342.763	405.272	479.431	567.377
27	28.83	30.821	32.987	35.344	40.71	47.084	54.669	63.706	74.484	87.351	102.723	121.1	143.079	169.374	200.841	238.499	283.569	337.502	402.032	479.221	571.522	681.853
28	29.975	32.129	34.481	37.051	42.931	49.968	58.403	68.528	80.698	95.339	112.968	134.21	159.817	190.699	227.95	272.889	327.104	392.503	471.378	566.481	681.112	819.223
29	31.124	33.45	35.999	38.792	45.219	52.966	62.323	73.64	87.347	103.966	124.135	148.631	178.397	214.583	258.583	312.094	377.17	456.303	552.512	669.447	811.523	984.068
30	32.28	34.785	37.539	40.568	47.575	56.085	66.439	79.058	94.461	113.283	136.308	164.494	199.021	241.333	293.199	356.787	434.745	530.312	647.439	790.948	966.712	1181.882
31	33.441	36.133	39.102	42.379	50.003	59.328	70.761	84.802	102.073	123.346	149.575	181.943	221.913	271.293	332.315	407.737	500.957	616.162	758.504	934.319	1151.387	1419.258
32	34.609	37.494	40.688	44.227	52.503	62.701	75.299	90.89	110.218	134.214	164.037	201.138	247.324	304.848	376.516	465.82	577.1	715.747	888.449	1103.496	1371.151	1704.109
33	35.782	38.869	42.299	46.112	55.078	66.21	80.064	97.343	118.933	145.951	179.8	222.252	275.529	342.429	426.463	532.035	664.666	831.267	1040.486	1303.125	1632.67	2045.931
34	36.961	40.258	43.933	48.034	57.73	69.858	85.067	104.184	128.259	158.627	196.982	245.477	306.837	384.521	482.903	607.52	765.365	965.27	1218.368	1538.688	1943.877	2456.118
35	38.145	41.66	45.592	49.994	60.462	73.652	90.32	111.435	138.237	172.317	215.711	271.024	341.59	431.663	546.681	693.573	881.17	1120.713	1426.491	1816.652	2314.214	2948.341
36	39.336	43.077	47.276	51.994	63.276	77.598	95.836	119.121	148.913	187.102	236.125	299.127	380.164	484.463	618.749	791.673	1014.346	1301.027	1669.994	2144.649	2754.914	3539.009
37	40.533	44.508	48.985	54.034	66.174	81.702	101.628	127.268	160.337	203.07	258.376	330.039	422.982	543.599	700.187	903.507	1167.498	1510.191	1954.894	2531.686	3279.348	4247.811
38	41.735	45.953	50.72	56.115	69.159	85.97	107.71	135.904	172.561	220.316	282.63	364.043	470.511	609.831	792.211	1030.998	1343.622	1752.822	2288.225	2988.389	3903.424	5098.373
39	42.944	47.412	52.481	58.237	72.234	90.409	114.095	145.058	185.64	238.941	309.066	401.448	523.267	684.01	896.198	1176.338	1546.165	2034.273	2678.224	3527.299	4646.075	6119.048
40	44.159	48.886	54.268	60.402	75.401	95.026	120.8	154.762	199.635	259.057	337.882	442.593	581.826	767.091	1013.704	1342.025	1779.09	2360.757	3134.522	4163.213	5529.829	7343.858
41	45.38	50.375	56.082	62.61	78.663	99.827	127.84	165.048	214.61	280.781	369.292	487.852	646.827	860.142	1146.486	1530.909	2046.954	2739.478	3668.391	4913.591	6581.496	8813.629
42	46.607	51.879	57.923	64.862	82.023	104.82	135.232	175.951	230.632	304.244	403.528	537.637	718.978	964.359	1296.529	1746.236	2354.997	3178.795	4293.017	5799.038	7832.981	10577.36
43	47.84	53.398	59.792	67.159	85.484	110.012	142.993	187.508	247.776	329.583	440.846	592.401	799.065	1081.083	1466.078	1991.709	2709.246	3688.402	5023.83	6843.865	9322.247	12693.83
44	49.079	54.932	61.689	69.503	89.048	115.413	151.143	199.758	266.121	356.95	481.522	652.641	887.963	1211.813	1657.668	2271.548	3116.633	4279.546	5878.881	8076.76	11094.47	15233.59
45	50.324	56.481	63.614	71.893	92.72	121.029	159.7	212.744	285.749	386.506	525.859	718.905	986.639	1358.23	1874.165	2590.565	3585.128	4965.274	6879.291	9531.577	13203.42	18281.31
46	51.576	58.046	65.568	74.331	96.501	126.871	168.685	226.508	306.752	418.426	574.186	791.795	1096.169	1522.218	2118.806	2954.244	4123.898	5760.718	8049.77	11248.26	15713.08	21938.57
47	52.834	59.626	67.552	76.817	100.397	132.945	178.119	241.099	329.224	452.9	626.863	871.975	1217.747	1705.884	2395.251	3368.838	4743.482	6683.433	9419.231	13273.95	18699.56	26327.29
48	54.098	61.223	69.565	79.354	104.408	139.263	188.025	256.565	353.27	490.132	684.28	960.172	1352.7	1911.59	2707.633	3841.475	5456.005	7753.782	11021.5	15664.26	22253.48	31593.74
49	55.368	62.835	71.609	81.941	108.541	145.834	198.427	272.958	378.999	530.343	746.866	1057.19	1502.497	2141.981	3060.626	4380.282	6275.405	8995.387	12896.16	18484.83	26482.64	37913.49
50	56.645	64.463	73.683	84.579	112.797	152.667	209.348	290.336	406.529	573.77	815.084	1163.909	1668.771	2400.018	3459.507	4994.521	7217.716	10435.65	15089.5	21813.09	31515.34	45497.19

	0.50%	1%	1.50%	2%	3%	4%	5%	6%	7%	8%	9%	10%	11%	12%	13%	14%	15%	16%	17%	18%	19%	20%
51	57.928	66.108	75.788	87.271	117.181	159.774	220.815	308.756	435.986	620.672	889.441	1281.299	1853.336	2689.02	3910.243	5694.754	8301.374	12106.35	17655.72	25740.45	37504.25	54597.63
52	59.218	67.769	77.925	90.016	121.696	167.165	232.856	328.281	467.505	671.326	970.491	1410.429	2058.203	3012.703	4419.575	6493.02	9547.58	14044.37	20658.19	30374.73	44631.06	65518.16
53	60.514	69.447	80.094	92.817	126.347	174.851	245.499	348.978	501.23	726.032	1058.835	1552.472	2285.605	3375.227	4995.119	7403.043	10980.72	16292.47	24171.08	35843.18	53111.96	78622.79
54	61.817	71.141	82.295	95.673	131.137	182.845	258.774	370.917	537.316	785.114	1155.13	1708.719	2538.022	3781.255	5645.485	8440.469	12628.82	18900.26	28281.17	42295.96	63204.23	94348.34
55	63.126	72.852	84.53	98.587	136.072	191.159	272.713	394.172	575.929	848.923	1260.092	1880.591	2818.204	4236.005	6380.398	9623.134	14524.15	21925.31	33069.96	49910.23	75214.04	113219
56	64.441	74.581	86.798	101.558	141.154	199.806	287.348	418.822	617.244	917.637	1374.5	2069.651	3129.207	4745.326	7210.85	10971.37	16703.77	25434.35	38716.26	58895.07	89505.7	135863.8
57	65.764	76.327	89.1	104.589	146.388	208.798	302.716	444.952	661.451	992.264	1499.205	2277.616	3474.419	5315.765	8149.26	12508.37	19210.34	29504.85	45299.02	69497.18	106512.8	163037.6
58	67.092	78.09	91.436	107.681	151.78	218.15	318.851	472.649	708.752	1072.645	1635.134	2506.377	3857.606	5954.656	9209.664	14260.54	22092.89	34226.63	53000.85	82007.68	126751.2	195646.1
59	68.428	79.871	93.808	110.835	157.333	227.876	335.794	502.008	759.365	1159.457	1783.296	2758.015	4282.942	6670.215	10407.92	16258.01	25407.82	39703.89	62012	96770.06	150834.9	234776.3
60	69.77	81.67	96.215	114.052	163.053	237.991	353.584	533.128	813.52	1253.213	1944.792	3034.816	4755.066	7471.641	11761.95	18535.13	29219.99	46057.51	72555.04	114189.7	179494.6	281732.6
	0.50%	1%	1.50%	2%	3%	4%	5%	6%	7%	8%	9%	10%	11%	12%	13%	14%	15%	16%	17%	18%	19%	20%
61	71.119	83.486	98.658	117.333	168.945	248.51	372.263	566.116	871.467	1354.47	2120.823	3339.298	5279.123	8369.238	13292	21131.05	33603.99	53427.71	84890.4	134744.8	213599.6	338080.1
62	72.474	85.321	101.138	120.679	175.013	259.451	391.876	601.083	933.469	1463.828	2312.698	3674.228	5860.827	9374.547	15020.96	24090.4	38645.59	61977.14	99322.76	158999.9	254184.5	405697.1
63	73.837	87.174	103.655	124.093	181.264	270.829	412.47	638.148	999.812	1581.934	2521.84	4042.651	6506.518	10500.49	16974.69	27464.06	44443.43	71894.49	116208.6	187620.8	302480.5	486837.5
64	75.206	89.046	106.21	127.575	187.702	282.662	434.093	677.437	1070.799	1709.489	2749.806	4447.916	7223.234	11761.55	19182.4	31310.02	51110.94	83398.6	135961.1	221393.6	359952.8	584006
65	76.582	90.937	108.803	131.126	194.333	294.968	456.798	719.083	1146.755	1847.248	2998.298	4893.707	8018.79	13173.94	21677.11	35694.43	58778.38	96743.38	159080.2	261245.4	428344.9	701048.2
66	77.965	92.846	111.435	134.749	201.163	307.767	480.636	763.228	1228.028	1996.028	3269.134	5384.078	8901.857	14755.81	24496.14	40692.65	67596.37	112223.3	186124.8	308270.6	509731.4	841258.9
67	79.355	94.774	114.106	138.444	208.198	321.078	505.67	810.022	1314.99	2156.71	3564.357	5923.486	9882.061	16527.51	27681.63	46390.62	77736.83	130180.1	217767	363760.3	606581.3	1009512
68	80.752	96.722	116.818	142.213	215.444	334.921	531.953	859.623	1408.039	2330.247	3886.149	6516.834	10970.09	18511.81	31281.24	52986.3	89398.35	151009.9	254788.4	429238.2	721832.8	1211415
69	82.155	98.689	119.57	146.057	222.907	349.318	559.551	912.2	1507.602	2517.667	4236.902	7169.518	12177.8	20734.23	35348.81	60291.39	102809.1	175172.4	298103.4	506502.1	859982	1453699
70	83.566	100.676	122.364	149.978	230.594	364.29	588.529	967.932	1614.134	2720.08	4619.223	7887.47	13518.36	23223.33	39945.15	68733.18	118231.5	203001	348782	597673.5	1022190	1744440
71	84.984	102.683	125.199	153.977	238.512	379.862	618.955	1027.008	1728.124	2938.686	5035.953	8577.217	15006.38	26011.13	45139.02	78356.82	135967.2	235714.2	408076	705255.7	1216407	2093329
72	86.409	104.71	128.077	158.057	246.667	396.057	650.903	1089.629	1850.092	3174.781	5490.189	9545.938	16658.08	29133.47	51008.09	89327.78	156363.3	273429.5	477449.9	832202.7	1447525	2511995
73	87.841	106.757	130.998	162.218	255.067	412.899	684.448	1156.006	1980.599	3429.764	5985.306	10501.53	18491.46	32630.48	57640.15	101834.7	179818.8	317179.2	558617.3	982000.2	1722556	3014396
74	89.28	108.825	133.963	166.463	263.719	430.415	719.67	1226.367	2120.241	3705.145	6524.984	11552.69	20526.53	36547.14	65134.36	116092.5	206792.6	367928.9	653583.3	1158676	2049842	3617276
75	90.727	110.913	136.973	170.792	272.631	448.631	756.654	1300.949	2269.657	4002.557	7113.232	12708.95	22785.44	40933.8	73602.83	132346.5	237812.5	426798.5	764693.4	1367339	2499313	4340732
76	92.18	113.022	140.027	175.208	281.81	467.577	795.486	1380.006	2429.533	4323.761	7754.423	13980.65	25292.84	45846.86	83172.2	150876	273485.5	495087.2	894692.3	1613461	2902784	5008879
77	93.641	115.152	143.128	179.712	291.264	487.28	836.261	1463.806	2600.601	4670.662	8453.321	15379.93	28076.06	51349.48	93985.59	171999.6	314509.1	574338.9	1046791	1903885	3454314	6250656
78	95.109	117.304	146.275	184.306	301.002	507.771	879.074	1552.634	2783.643	5045.315	9215.12	16918.31	31165.42	57512.41	106204.7	196080.6	361686.5	666191.5	1224747	2244586	4110634	7500798
79	96.585	119.477	149.469	188.992	311.032	529.082	924.027	1646.792	2979.498	5449.94	10045.48	18611.82	34594.62	64414.9	120012.3	223532.8	415940.5	772783.2	1432954	2650972	4891656	9000947

Age	0.5%	1%	1.50%	2%	3%	4%	5%	6%	7%	8%	9%	10%	11%	12%	13%	14%	15%	16%	17%	18%	19%	20%
80	98.068	121.672	152.711	193.772	321.363	551.245	971.229	1746.6	3189.063	5886.935	10950.57	20474	38401.03	72145.69	136614.9	254828.4	478332.5	896429.5	1676558	3128480	5821071	1060.1137
81	99.558	123.888	156.002	198.647	332.004	574.295	1020.79	1852.396	3413.297	6358.89	11937.13	22522.4	42626.14	80804.18	153245.9	290505.4	550083.4	1039859	1961573	3691216	6927076	1296.1366
82	101.056	126.127	159.342	203.62	342.964	598.267	1072.83	1964.54	3653.228	6868.601	13012.47	24775.64	47316.601	90501.68	1731688	3311772	632596.9	1206238	2295042	4355636	8243221	1555.3640
83	102.561	128.388	162.732	208.693	354.253	623.197	1127.471	2083.412	3909.954	7419.09	14184.59	27254.21	52521.77	1013629	195681.8	377543	727487.5	1399237	2685200	5139651	9809434	1866.4369
84	104.074	130.672	166.173	213.867	365.881	649.125	1184.845	2209.417	4184.651	8013.617	15462.2	29980.63	58380.17	113527.4	221121.4	430400	836611.6	1623116	3141685	6004789	11673228	2239.7244
85	105.594	132.979	169.665	219.144	377.857	676.09	1245.087	2342.982	4478.576	8655.706	16854.8	32979.69	64714.19	127151.7	249868.2	490657	962104.3	1882815	3675773	7156452	13891142	2687.6693
86	107.122	135.309	173.21	224.527	390.193	704.134	1308.341	2484.561	4793.076	9349.163	18372.73	36278.66	71833.75	142409.9	282352.1	559350	1106421	2184066	4300655	8444615	16530460	3225.2033
87	108.658	137.662	176.808	230.017	402.898	733.299	1374.758	2634.634	5129.592	10098.1	20027.28	39907.53	79736.46	159501.2	319058.8	637640	1272385	2533518	5031767	9964646	19671248	3870.2441
88	110.201	140.036	180.46	235.618	415.985	763.631	1444.496	2793.712	5489.663	10906.94	21830.73	43899.28	88508.47	178642.4	360537.5	726933.4	1463244	2938882	5887169	11758204	23408787	4644.2930
89	111.752	142.439	184.167	241.33	429.465	795.176	1517.721	2962.335	5874.94	11780.5	23796.5	48290.21	98245.4	200080.5	407408.3	828705.1	1682731	3409104	6887988	13874776	27856457	5573.1517
90	113.311	144.863	187.93	247.157	443.349	827.983	1594.607	3141.075	6287.185	12723.94	25939.18	53130.23	109053.4	224091.1	460372.4	944724.8	1935142	3954562	8056947	16372236	33149185	6687.7821
91	114.877	147.312	191.749	253.1	457.649	862.103	1675.338	3330.54	6728.298	13742.85	28274.71	58433.25	121050.3	250983.1	520221.8	1076987	2225414	4587293	9428969	19319240	39447531	8025.3386
92	116.452	149.765	195.625	259.162	472.379	897.587	1760.105	3531.372	7200.269	14843.28	30820.44	64277.57	134366.8	281102	587851.7	1227764	2559228	5321260	11031895	22796704	46942563	9630.4063
93	118.034	152.283	199.559	265.345	487.55	934.49	1849.11	3744.254	7705.287	16031.75	33595.27	70706.33	149148.2	314835.3	664273.4	1399655	2943113	6172663	12907318	26900112	55861651	1.16E+08
94	119.624	154.806	203.553	271.652	503.177	972.87	1942.565	3969.91	8245.658	17315.28	36619.85	77777.96	165555.4	352616.5	756629.9	1595607	3384581	7162090	15101564	31742133	66475366	1.39E+08
95	121.222	157.354	207.606	278.085	519.272	1012.785	2040.694	4209.104	8823.854	18701.51	39916.64	85556.76	183767.5	394931.5	848212.8	1818993	3892269	8308938	17668830	37455718	79105686	1.66E+08
96	122.829	159.927	211.72	284.647	535.85	1054.296	2143.728	4462.651	9442.523	20198.63	43510.13	94113.44	203983	442304.2	958481.5	2073654	4476110	9634899	20672532	44197748	94135768	2E+08
97	124.443	162.527	215.896	291.34	552.926	1097.468	2251.915	4731.41	10104.5	21815.52	47427.04	103525.8	226422.1	495404.2	1080085	2363966	5147528	11176472	24186864	52153344	1.12E+08	2.4E+08
98	126.065	165.152	220.134	298.166	570.513	1142.367	2365.51	5016.294	10812.82	23561.76	51696.48	113879.4	251329.5	554853.7	1223887	2694922	5919658	12964708	28298632	61540947	1.33E+08	2.88E+08
99	127.695	167.803	224.436	305.13	588.629	1189.061	2484.786	5318.272	11570.71	25447.7	56350.16	125268.3	278876.8	621437.1	1382993	3072212	6807608	15039063	33109400	72618318	1.59E+08	3.45E+08
100	129.334	170.481	228.803	312.232	607.288	1237.624	2610.025	5638.368	12381.66	27484.52	61422.68	137796.1	309665.2	696010.5	1562784	3502323	7828750	17445314	38737999	85689616	1.89E+08	4.14E+08

APPENDIX D
Mortgage Checklist

The mortgage checklist (link at the bottom of the page) is from a leading real estate web site – Zillow.com.

Zillow provides information and tools that help consumers make smart decisions about homes, real estate and mortgages.

According to their web site:

What We Do

Zillow is a home and real estate marketplace dedicated to helping homeowners, buyers, sellers, renters, real estate agents, mortgage professionals, landlords and property managers find and share vital information about homes, real estate and mortgages. We are transforming the way consumers make home-related decisions and connect with real estate professionals.

It starts with our living database of more than 100 million U.S. homes - including homes for sale, homes for rent and homes not currently on the market. Add to that Zestimate® home values, Rent Zestimates and lots of other useful information you won't find anywhere else, and as a result, consumers are given an edge in real estate.

In addition to Zillow.com, we also operate Zillow Mortgage Marketplace, where borrowers connect with lenders to find loans and get the best mortgage rates; and Zillow Mobile, the most popular real estate mobile platform today.

The following link is to Zillow's informative Mortgage Checklist page.

http://www.zillow.com/mortgage/help/Mortgage-Checklist.htm

APPENDIX E
RESIDENTIAL HOUSE LEASE AGREEMENT

This Residential House Lease Agreement ("Lease") is made and effective this **[ENTER CURRENT DATE HERE]** by and between **George Smith** ("Landlord") and **Eddie Wycowsky** and **[Tenant Two]** ("Tenant," whether one or more). This Lease creates joint and several liability in the case of multiple Tenants.

1. **PREMISES**.
Landlord hereby rents to Tenant and Tenant accepts in its present condition the house at following address: **1525 Broadway, [ENTER STUDENT'S TOWN AND STATE HERE]** (the "House").

2. **TERM**.
The term of this Lease shall start on **[1 WEEK FROM CURRENT Date PLUS FIVE YEARS]**, and end on **[1 WEEK AND SIX MONTHS AND FIVE YEARS FROM CURRENT Date]**. In the event that Landlord is unable to provide the House on the exact start date, then Landlord shall provide the House as soon as possible, and Tenant's is not obligated to pay rent during such period.

3. **RENT**.
Tenant agrees to pay, without demand, to Landlord as rent for the House the sum of **$800.00** per month in advance on the first day of each calendar month, at such place as Landlord may designate. Landlord may impose a late payment charge of **$50** per day for any amount that is

165

more than five (5) days late. Rent will be prorated if the term does not start on the first day of the month or for any other partial month of the term.

4. **SECURITY DEPOSIT**.

Upon execution of this Lease, Tenant deposits with Landlord **$800**, as security for the performance by Tenant of the terms of this Lease to be returned to Tenant, without interest, following the full and faithful performance by Tenant of this Lease. In the event of damage to the House caused by Tenant or Tenant's family, agents or visitors, Landlord may use funds from the deposit to repair, but is not limited to this fund and Tenant remains liable.

5. **QUIET ENJOYMENT**.

Landlord agrees that if Tenant timely pays the rent and performs the other obligations in this Lease, Landlord will not interfere with Tenant's peaceful use and enjoyment of the House.

6. **USE OF PREMISES**.

Tenant shall comply with all the health and sanitary laws, ordinances, rules, and orders of appropriate governmental authorities and homes associations, if any, with respect to the House.

7. **NUMBER OF OCCUPANTS**.

Tenant agrees that the House shall be occupied by no more than **4** persons without the prior written consent of Landlord.

8. **CONDITION OF PREMISES**.

Tenant agrees that Tenant has examined the House, including the grounds and all buildings and improvements, and that they are, at the time of this Lease, in good order, good repair, safe, clean, and tenantable condition.

9. **ASSIGNMENT AND SUBLETTING**.

A. Tenant shall not assign this Lease, or sublet the House or any part of the House without Landlord's prior written consent.

B. Any assignment, or subletting without the prior written consent of Landlord, or an assignment or subletting by operation of law, shall be void and, at Landlord's option, terminate this Lease.

10. **ALTERATIONS AND IMPROVEMENTS**.

A. Tenant shall make no alterations to the House or construct any building or make other improvements without the prior written consent of Landlord.

B. All alterations, changes, and improvements built, constructed, or placed on or around the House by Tenant, with the exception of fixtures properly removable without damage to the House and movable personal property, shall, unless otherwise provided by written agreement between Landlord and Tenant, be the property of Landlord and remain at the expiration or earlier termination of this Lease.

11. **DAMAGE TO PREMISES**.

If the House, or any part of the House, shall be partially damaged by fire or other casualty not due to Tenant's negligence or willful act, or that of Tenant's family, agent, or visitor, there shall be an abatement of rent corresponding with the time during which, and the extent to which, the House is untenantable. If Landlord shall decide not to rebuild or repair, the term of this Lease shall end and the rent shall be prorated up to the time of the damage.

12. **DANGEROUS MATERIALS**.

Tenant shall not keep or have on or around the House any article or thing of a dangerous, inflammable, or explosive character that might unreasonably increase the danger of fire on or around the House or that might be considered hazardous.

13. **UTILITIES**.

Tenant shall be responsible for arranging and paying for all utility services required on the premises. Tenant shall not default on any obligation to a utility provider for utility services at the House.

14. **MAINTENANCE AND REPAIR**.

A. Tenant will, at Tenant's sole expense, keep and maintain the House and appurtenances in good and sanitary condition and repair during the term of this Lease. In particular, Tenant shall keep the fixtures in the House in good order and repair; keep the furnace clean; and keep the walks free from dirt and debris. Tenant shall, at Tenant's sole expense, make all required repairs to the plumbing, range, oven heating apparatus, electric and gas fixtures, other mechanical devices and systems, floors, ceilings and walls whenever damage to such items shall have resulted from Tenant's misuse, waste, or neglect, or that of the Tenant's family, agent, or visitor.

B. Tenant agrees that no signs shall be placed or painting done on or about the House by Tenant without the prior written consent of Landlord.

C. Tenant agrees to promptly notify Landlord in the event of any damage, defect or destruction of the House, or the failure of any of Landlord's appliances or mechanical systems, and except for repairs or replacements that are the obligation of Tenant pursuant to Subsection A above, Landlord shall use its best efforts to repair or replace such damaged or defective area, appliance or mechanical system.

15. **ANIMALS**.
Tenant shall keep no domestic or other animals in or about the House without the prior written consent of Landlord.

16. **RIGHT OF INSPECTION**.
Landlord and Landlord's agents shall have the right at all reasonable times during the term of this Lease and any renewal of this Lease to enter the House for the purpose of inspecting the premises and/or making any repairs to the premises or other item as required under this Lease.

17. **DISPLAY OF SIGNS**.

During the last thirty (30) days of this Lease, Landlord or Landlord's agent may display "For Sale" or "For Rent" or "Vacancy" or similar signs on or about the House and enter to show the House to prospective purchasers or tenants.

18. **HOLDOVER BY TENANT**.

Should Tenant remain in possession of the House with the consent of Landlord after the expiration of the Term of this Lease, a new tenancy from month to month shall be created which shall be subject to all the terms and conditions of this Lease, but shall be terminable on thirty (30) days by either party or longer notice if required by law. If Tenant holds over without Landlord's consent, Landlord is entitled to double rent, pro-rated per each day of the holdover, lasting until Tenant leaves the House.

19. **SURRENDER OF PREMISES**.

At the expiration of the Lease, Tenant shall quit and surrender the House in as good a condition as it was at the commencement of this Lease, reasonable wear and tear and damages by the elements excepted.

20. **FORFEITURE OF SECURITY DEPOSIT - DEFAULT**.

It is understood and agreed that Tenant shall not attempt to apply or deduct any portion of any security deposit from the last or any month's rent or use or apply any such security deposit at any time in lieu of payment of rent. If Tenant fails to comply, such security deposit shall be forfeited and Landlord may recover the rent due as if any such deposit had not been applied or deducted from the rent due. Furthermore, any deposit shall be held as a guarantee that Tenant shall perform the obligations of the Lease and shall be forfeited by the Tenant should Tenant breach any of the terms and conditions of this Lease. In the event of default, by Tenant, of any obligation in this Lease which is not cured by Tenant within fifteen (15) days notice from Landlord, then in addition to forfeiture of the Security Deposit, Landlord may pursue any other remedy available at law.

21. **ABANDONMENT**.

If at any time during the term of this Lease, Tenant abandons the House or any of Tenant's personal property in or about the House, Landlord shall have the following rights: Landlord may, at Landlord's option, enter the House by any means without liability to Tenant for damages and may relet the House, for the whole or any part of the term, and may collect all rent payable; Also, at Landlord's option, Landlord may hold Tenant liable for any difference between the rent that would have been payable under this Lease during the balance of the unexpired term, if this Lease had continued in force, and the net rent for such period realized by Landlord by means of such reletting. Landlord may also dispose of any of Tenant's abandoned personal property as Landlord deems appropriate, without liability to Tenant. Landlord is entitled to presume that Tenant has abandoned the House if Tenant removes substantially all of Tenant's furnishings from the House, if the House is unoccupied for a period of two (2) consecutive weeks, or if it would otherwise be reasonable for Landlord to presume under the circumstances that the Tenant has abandoned the House.

22. **SECURITY**.

Tenant acknowledges that Landlord does not provide a security alarm system or any security for the House or for Tenant and that any such alarm system or security service, if provided, is not represented or warranted to be complete in all respects or to protect Tenant from all harm. Tenant hereby releases Landlord from any loss, suit, claim, charge, damage or injury resulting from lack of security or failure of security.

23. **SEVERABILITY**.

If any part or parts of this Lease shall be held unenforceable for any reason, the remainder of this Agreement shall continue in full force and effect.

24. **INSURANCE**.

Tenant acknowledges that Landlord will not provide insurance coverage for Tenant's property, nor shall Landlord be responsible for any loss of Tenant's property, whether by theft, fire, acts of God, or otherwise.

25. **BINDING EFFECT**.

The covenants and conditions contained in the Lease shall apply to and bind the heirs, legal representatives, and permitted assigns of the parties.

26. **GOVERNING LAW**.

It is agreed that this Lease shall be governed by, construed, and enforced in accordance with the laws of the State of **[student's state]**

27. **ENTIRE AGREEMENT**.

This Lease shall constitute the entire agreement between the parties. Any prior understanding or representation of any kind preceding the date of this Lease is hereby superseded. This Lease may be modified only by a writing signed by both Landlord and Tenant.

28. **NOTICES**.

Any notice required or otherwise given pursuant to this Lease shall be in writing; hand delivered, mailed certified return receipt requested, postage prepaid, or delivered by overnight delivery service, if to Tenant, at the House and if to Landlord, at the address for payment of rent.

IN WITNESS WHEREOF, the parties have caused this Lease to be executed the day and year first above written.

[Signature]

APPENDIX F
Sample Investment Account Applications (Links)
& other information

IRA Application:

American Century
https://www.americancentury.com/pdf/account
applications/roth_ira_app.pdf

Mutual Fund Application:

Tocqueville
www.tocqueville.com/sites/default/files/Regular
Application_0.pdf

Brokerage Account Application:

Charles Schwab
www.schwab.com/public/schwab/investing/accounts
products/accounts

Mutual Fund Companies:

Vanguard: www.vanguard.com
Fidelity Investments: www.fidelity.com
Others: http://en.wikipedia.org/wiki/List
of_mutual-fund_families_in_the_United_States

Online Brokerage Companies:

E*Trade: www.etrade.com
Scottrade: www.scottrade.com
TD Ameritrade: www.tdameritrade.com
Interactive Brokers: www.interactivebrokers.com
Options Express: www.optionsexpress.com
TradeStation: www.tradestation.com

Full-Service Investment Firms:

JP Morgan Securities
Morgan Stanley/Smith Barney
Bank of America/Merrill Lynch
Edward Jones
Raymond James

Morningstar Fund Ratings: www.morningstar.com/Cover/Funds.aspx

(Mutual Funds and more)

J.D. Power Ratings Viewer: www.jdpower.com/consumer-ratings/ratings.htm

(Select Finance Industry and then narrow by Category and Rating)

APPENDIX G

To view historical and current portfolios online go to www.4tnoxu.com.

4t Nox U is a new personal finance web site dedicated to knowledge and application. Its goal is to provide streamlined information that is applicable and actionable. In a world of data overload, it is helpful to have simple, concise, actionable information.

Static portfolios are free to the general public as well as a bevy of other related topical information.

Memberships will soon be available in two tiers:

1) Premium – Access to three actively-managed portfolios (growth, balanced, income)

2) Gold – Access to an active trading account, prop research and more.

The 4t Nox U mission is to find, create and disseminate practical, applicable information through a filter that reduces unnecessary complexity and noise and drives action. The question asked most often by non-professional investors is, "So what?" The expanded versions are "so what does that mean," so what benefit is that to me," and "so what am I to do next?"

4t Nox U is not an advisor, and therefore will not offer particular advice of any kind, but it will provide answers to those universal questions. Consumers are at liberty to use (or not use) whatever information they deem applicable to their distinct situation. Hopefully the U's resources will be valuable to our members when they need them most – the utility of on-demand learning via the internet.

E-LINKS

Listed as they appear in the text.

Discussion 2:

    2.1

Economic Value of Education:
http://www.census.gov/prod/2002pubs/p23-210.pdf
College Remediation:
http://www.usatoday.com/news/education/2008-09-15-
Colleges-remedialclasses_N.htm
Student Loan Debt:
http://online.wsj.com/article/SB10001424052702303812904
577295930047604846.html?mod=googlenews_wsj
Man in the Arena:
http://www.theodoreroosevelt.org/life/quotes.htm

    2.2

Social Contract Theory (Locke v. Hobbes):
http://www.iep.utm.edu/soc-cont/
Starbucks Marketing (slides):
http://www.slideshare.net/sk_prince/starbucks-
international-marketing-strategy-3900413

    2.4

Poetry Forum: http://www.pmpoetry.com/forums.shtml
Poetry Publishing: http://www.poetry-publishers.com/
Web Sites: http://www.web.com/
Self-Publishing: https://www.createspace.com/

On-line Payments: https://www.paypal.com/
Customer Surveys: http://www.surveymonkey.com/
Edgar Allan Poe: http://www.poemuseum.org/index.php

Discussion 3:
    3.1
Budget Link: http://www.4tnoxu.com/

Discussion 4:
    4.3
Personal Finance Web Site: http://www.4tnoxu.com/
Mutual Fund Companies:
https://www.fidelity.com/
https://personal.vanguard.com/us/CorporatePortal
https://www.americancentury.com/index.jsp
https://www.schwab.com/public/schwab/investing

    4.4
Personal Finance Web Sites:
http://www.forbes.com/fdc/welcome_mjx.shtml
http://www.kiplinger.com/
http://www.investors.com/introad.aspx
http://www.4tnoxu.com/
http://www.fool.com/
http://www.thestreet.com/
http://www.minyanville.com/

Discussion 5:
    5.1

Gov't Protection v. Gov't Bureaucracy:
http://www.foxnews.com/politics/2012/03/21/supreme-court-sides-with-idaho-property-owners-over-epa/

5.3
Madness of Crowds:
http://www.amazon.com/Extraordinary-Popular-Delusions-Madness-Crowds/dp/051788433X

Discussion 6:
6.1
Berkshire Hathaway Inc.:
http://www.berkshirehathaway.com/
Tax Code Complexity:
http://www.irs.gov/pub/irs-utl/08_tas_arc_intro_toc_msp.pdf
National Taxpayer Advocate:
http://www.irs.gov/advocate/
Marginal Tax Rate Chart:
http://www.taxfoundation.org/research/show/27323.html
Federal Income Taxpayer Chart:
http://www.taxpolicycenter.org/taxtopics/federal-taxes-households.cfm
Public Search Engine: http://www.google.com/
Private Search Engine: https://www.ixquick.com/

6.2
Auto Insurance: http://www.autoinsurancequotes.com/
Term Life Insurance: http://www.intelliquote.com/

6.3
Insurance Web Sites:
Health: http://www.ehealthinsurance.com/
Life: http://www.intelliquote.com/
Disability: http://www2.iii.org/individuals/disabilityinsurance/
Automobile: http://www.autoinsurancequotes.com/
Homeowners/Renters: http://www.iii.org/individuals/homei/
Umbrella: http://en.wikipedia.org/wiki/Umbrella_insurance

Discussion 7:
"Live Free Or Die; Death Is Not The Worst Of Evils":
http://www.nh.gov/nhinfo/emblem.html

Martin Luther King, Jr. Commencement Address:
http://www.oberlin.edu/external/EOG/BlackHistoryMonth/
MLK/CommAddress.html

Resources: http://www.4tnoxu.com/
http://www.4tnox.com

Debt Warning:

U.S. Debt Clock: http://www.usdebtclock.org/
Median & Per Capita Household Incomes:
http://quickfacts.census.gov/qfd/states/00000.html
Federal Income Taxpayer Chart:
http://www.taxpolicycenter.org/taxtopics/federal-taxes-
households.cfm
Federal Budget Tables (2.2):
http://www.whitehouse.gov/omb/budget/historicals

Federal Unfunded Obligations:
http://blog.heritage.org/2011/06/07/governments-unfunded-obligations-now-total-534000-per-household/
Federal Budget Deficit:
http://www.concordcoalition.org/issues/indicators/snapshot-spending-revenue-and-deficit
Federal Budget Tables (1.1):
http://www.whitehouse.gov/omb/budget/historicals
Federal Unfunded Obligations:
http://www.usatoday.com/news/washington/2011-06-06-us-owes-62-trillion-in-debt_n.htm?loc=interstitialskip
Federal Budget Tables (7.1):
http://www.whitehouse.gov/omb/budget/historicals
Thomas Jefferson Quote (Dangerous Banking Establishments):
http://www.monticello.org/site/jefferson/private-banks-quotation
Thomas Jefferson Quote (Mortgaging Posterity):
http://www.memory.loc.gov/master/mss/mtj/mtj1/052/0400/0403.jpg

Glossary:

Federal Reserve:
http://www.federalreserve.gov/faqs/about_12594.htm

Critic 1:
http://www.amazon.com/End-Fed-Ron-Paul/dp/0446549193

Critic 2: http://www.amazon.com/The-Creature-Jekyll-Island-Federal/dp/091298645X/ref=sr_1_2?ie=UTF8&qid=13329553255&sr=8-2

GLOSSARY

* 10-K = A comprehensive report of a company's history, organizational structure, equity, holdings, subsidiaries, financial statements, performance, etc. that must be submitted annually to the Securities and Exchange Commission. The 10-K must be filed within 60 days of fiscal year end.

* 10-Q = Similar report as the 10-K, but filed quarterly, within 35 days after each of the first three fiscal quarters ends.

* 401(k) = The name 401(k) comes from the IRS section describing the program. It is a defined contribution plan (as compared to a "defined benefit" plan) offered by corporations to their employees. Employees can set aside tax-deferred income into this program for retirement purposes, and in some cases employers will match contributions up to a certain amount.

* 403(b) = The name 403(b) comes from the IRS section describing the program. It is a defined contribution plan offered by non-profit organizations to their employees. Employees can set aside tax-deferred income into this program for retirement purposes. Organizations do not match contributions.

* Alpha = A risk-adjusted measure of the active return on an investment. Positive alpha is the abnormal rate of return on a security or portfolio in excess of what would be predicted by an equilibrium model like CAPM. It is the return in excess of the compensation for the risk borne, and thus commonly used to assess active managers' performances.

* Balance Sheet = A financial statement that summarizes a company's assets, liabilities and shareholder's equity at a specific point in time.

* Beta = A historical measure which describes the correlation of the returns of a stock or portfolio with those of the stock market (benchmark index) as a whole.

* Blue-chip Stocks = A well-established, financially-sound corporation with a national reputation for quality and reliability and that has the ability to operate profitably in good times and bad.

* Cash Flow = A revenue or expense stream that changes a cash account over a given period. As an accounting statement – the statement of cash flows – the amount of cash generated and used by a company in a given period of time.

* CFPB = Consumer Finance Protection Bureau. Established by the Consumer Protection Act of 2010. The central mission of the CFPB is to make markets for consumer financial products and services work for Americans – whether they are applying for a mortgage, choosing among credit cards, or using any number of other consumer financial products.

* Commodities = A basic good used in commerce that is interchangeable with other commodities of the same type.

Commodities are most often used as inputs in the production of other goods and services – corn, wheat, cattle, pigs, etc.

* Convexity = A measure of the sensitivity of the duration of a bond to changes in interest rates, the second derivative of the price of the bond with respect to interest rates. Convexity is used as a risk-management tool, and helps to measure and manage the amount of market risk to which a portfolio of bonds is exposed.

* EBITDA = Earnings Before Interest, Taxes, Depreciation & Amortization. This earnings figure is used to measure (and compare between companies and industries) a company's operating profitability because it eliminates the effects of financing and accounting decisions.

* FDIC = Federal Deposit Insurance Corporation. The FDIC is an independent agency created by Congress to maintain stability and public confidence in the nation's financial system by: insuring deposits; examining and supervising financial institutions for safety and soundness and consumer protection; managing receiverships.

* Federal Reserve = The Central Bank of the United States. www.federalreserve.gov/faqs/about_12594.htm (on the other side, a critic or two...)

* Financial Statements = Records that outline the financial activities of a business, an individual or any other entity. They are meant to present financial information as clearly and concisely as possible for both the entity and its readers. Financial statements for businesses usually include: an income statement; a balance sheet; and a statement of cash flows.

* **FINRA** = Financial Industry Regulatory Authority. FINRA is the largest independent regulator for all securities firms doing business in the United States. It oversees nearly 4,435 brokerage firms, 161,450 branch offices, and 630,155 registered securities representatives. Its chief role is to protect investors by maintaining the fairness of the U.S. capital markets.

* **Fiscal Policy** = Government expenditures and revenue collections. Fiscal policy has broad affects on individuals, companies, and organizations, and, consequently, it has an effect on the economy.

* **Futures** = A derivative contract obligating the buyer to purchase an asset and the seller to sell an asset, such as a physical commodity or financial instrument, at a predetermined future date and price. Futures contracts detail the quality and quantity of the underlying asset and are traded on futures exchanges.

* **GDP** = Gross Domestic Product. The market value of all officially recognized final goods and services produced within a country in a given period. GDP = Consumption + Investment + Government Spending + Net Exports.

* **Hedge Fund** = An investment fund that can undertake a wider range of investment and trading activities than other funds, but which is only open for investment from particular

types of investors; institutions, pension funds, university endowments, foundations, high-net worth individuals, and sophisticated investors.

* **Income Statement** = A summary of a business' revenues and expenses (both operating and non-operating activities) which shows the net profit/loss incurred over a specified accounting period (monthly, quarterly, annually).

* **IRA** = Individual Retirement Account. There are several types of IRAs: Traditional, Roth, SIMPLE, SEP, etc. A form of a retirement plan in the United States that provides tax advantages for retirement saving/investing.

* **Market Capitalization** = The total value of a company's equity in dollar terms (Price per share X number of shares outstanding)

    Micro-cap - Under $250 million (MM) in market cap.
    Small-cap - $250MM - $1 billion (B)
    Mid-cap - $1B - $5B
    Large-cap – Over $5B
    Mega-cap – Over $100B

* **Monetary Policy** = The process by which the monetary authority of a country controls the supply of money, often targeting a rate of interest for the purpose of promoting economic growth and stability. In the U.S., the Fed has a dual mandate of promoting both maximum employment and stable prices.

5555555555

* **Options =** A derivative financial instrument that conveys the right, but not the obligation, to engage in a future transaction.

* **Price-to-Book Ratio =** The P/B ratio is a financial ratio used to compare a company's book value to its current market price. When intangible assets and goodwill are excluded, the ratio is often specified as "price to tangible book."

* **Price-to-Earnings Ratio =** The P/E ratio is a financial ratio used to measure the price paid for a share relative to the annual net income per share earned by the company.

* **SEC =** Securities and Exchange Commission. The mission of the U.S. SEC is to protect investors, maintain fair, orderly, and efficient markets, and facilitate capital formation.

www.ingramcontent.com/pod-product-compliance
Lightning Source LLC
Chambersburg PA
CBHW060020210326
41520CB00009B/943